Gardening *from a* Hammock

ADVICE FROM GARDEN EXPERTS ON EASY-CARE PLANTS

Ellen Novack and Dan Cooper

How to create a low-maintenance garden

First edition January 2012
Second printing May 2015

Library and Archives Canada Cataloguing in Publication

Novack, Ellen
      Gardening from a hammock : low-maintenance gardening / Ellen Novack and Dan Cooper.

Edited by Wendy Thomas

Book Design by TTC Creative Communication

Front cover photograph by Dan Cooper

Includes index.
ISBN 978-0-9877664-0-3

      1. Low maintenance gardening.   2. Gardening.
      3. Plants, Ornamental.   I. Cooper, Dan (Dan A.) II. Title.

SB473.N68 2011   635.9   C2011-907273-4

All inquiries may be addressed to *gardeningfromahammock@rogers.com*

Printed in Canada

Table of Contents

Caryopteris 'Summer Sorbet'

In Praise of our Gardeners

We would like to thank the creative gardeners who we interviewed for sharing their expertise, time and love of gardening. It is because of their long hours, hard work and devotion to gardening that we can learn to have more time and less work with beautiful results in our own gardens.

With much gratitude and appreciation to:
Aldona Satterthwaite, Belinda Gallagher, Dugald Cameron, Frank Kershaw, Jim Lounsbery, Katy Anderson, Kim Price, Lindsay Dale-Harris, Lorraine Flanigan, Marion Jarvie, Marjorie and Jeff Mason, Martin Galloway, Mary Fisher, Merle Burston, Paul Zammit, Sonia Leslie, and Susan Lipchak.

Dedications

Dedicated to Bernard Novack (1912–2010) – Bernard Novack, a man who always had a smile on his face, a story to tell and a song to sing. A man who loved the sun, and was the sun to so many.

A special thanks to my mother, **Diane Novack**, not only for reading and commenting on every chapter, but also for inspiring my love of gardening by creating lasting memories of fragrant lilacs and sunshine forsythia on the path to our front door.

And, as always, love and appreciation to my husband, **John Park**, for lugging around soil, digging holes in hard clay, fixing hoses and moving plants from one spot to another, when what he really loves about gardening is sitting in the hammock with a beer and a book.

Ellen Novack

I would like to dedicate this book to my fellow **Toronto Master Gardeners** for their assistance in creating this book and for their contribution to sharing gardening knowledge with the public.

I should also dedicate this to the **Toronto Botanical Garden** and, in particular **Paul Zammit** and **Aldona Satterthwaite**, for all of their help in introducing the gardening world to the wonders of gardening.

Dan Cooper

Gardening from a Hammock

Introduction

Gardening from a Hammock is a practical, simple and useful guide for new gardeners, busy gardeners, and avid gardeners seeking new ideas for low maintenance gardening.

This book is for those of us who love to garden, but have neither the time, knowledge nor energy to do much about it. This book is for those of us who, try as we may, can't quite get the perennials to bloom so we have colour all season, never mind winter interest. It is for those of us who, despite our best intentions to water, weed, prune and divide, don't.

Why this book?

Because it provides expert tips for the lazy gardener. You will learn tips to save time, ways to conserve water and techniques to avoid weeding. You will discover plants that will survive benign neglect; the easy-care stars of the plant world.

We asked experts to tell us how to plant a low-maintenance garden that will look good all year. Some of these experts are master gardeners, some professional landscapers, some teachers and lecturers and some nursery owners. One thing they have in common is that they all love plants and none of them is a lazy gardener. But they can help you become one.

We let them pick their favourite low-maintenance shade and sun plants. Some experts recommended colour combinations and tips on creating attractive shade gardens using only leaf colours, shapes and textures. Others provided specific combinations of plants that work particularly well together to create dramatic impact.

word
bout soil

of the few things
all the experts agree
is that soil is the
bone of any garden.
e soil isn't right, your
n won't thrive. Good
eeds your plants for
Add lots of compost
our reward will be
ficantly healthier
s with less work the
f the season.

Keep in mind, however, that low maintenance does not mean no maintenance. Plants are alive and, like all living things, require some care and nurturing – unless your plants are plastic.

How to use this book

Our gardening experts explain the reasons why they chose each individual plant, and what they most admire about it.

We have divided their choices into specific garden styles so that you can browse and decide which has the most appeal: a white garden, an aristocratic garden, a tall dancing garden, a drought tolerant garden or any one of the 17 different choices. Readers also can mix and match plant combinations from several gardens to customize their own.

To further assist in choosing a low-maintenance garden, we have an extensive plant chart at the back of the book. This includes most of the plants mentioned in the chapters with information about their height, spacing, bloom time, colour, hardiness and how to use them.

Botanical names are important because some plants have many common names and if you relied on the common name you might end up buying the wrong plant.

If you see a plant that you like in a chapter, refer to the chart at the back of the book to read a description of it and see its photo. Each of the plants is listed by its botanical name. Botanical names are important because some plants have many common names and if you relied on the common name you might end up buying the wrong plant. All reputable nurseries should be using the same botanical names.

Enjoy your browsing and then take this book with its photos and botanical names to your local nursery to select your favourite combinations. Plant, water, and then enjoy swinging in your hammock while admiring your low-maintenance garden.

To Water or not to Water? That is the question

If planning for a low-maintenance garden that has non-stop interest year round isn't complicated enough, the expert gardeners had very different takes on how we should water.

There is a definite and practical trend toward reducing supplemental watering. The gardeners had a variety of ways to limit watering, including trough gardens and xeriscaping.

Martin Galloway, for instance, does not water any of his plants in his 17-acre nursery. As a botanist he explains that plants grown without additional water develop different tissues to adapt (see the Naturalist Garden chapter). Belinda Gallagher (see the Sustainable Garden chapter) says that as the weather becomes more extreme, we need to respond to it with more drought-tolerant gardening and make sustainable choices. At Mason House Gardens, Jeff and Marjorie Mason practice xeriscaping, initially because they found themselves on sandy soil without a working well, and now because it works (check out the Xeriscape Garden).

Top Ten Plants

These are the most frequently chosen low-maintenance plants selected by our gardening experts:

Acer griseum (Paperbark maple)

Adiantum pedatum (Maidenhair fern)

Alchemilla mollis (Lady's mantle)

Athyrium niponicum 'Pictum' (Japanese painted fern)

Carex morrowii 'Ice Dance' (Creeping Japanese sedge)

Cornus alternifolia 'Golden Shadows' ('Golden Shadows' pagoda dogwood)

Epimedium (Barrenwort – any and all)

Hakonechloa macra 'Aureola' (Golden Japanese forest grass)

Hosta 'June' (Hosta)

Geranium 'Rozanne' (Cranesbill geranium 'Rozanne')

Alchemilla mollis 'Lady's mantle'

Athyrium niponicum 'Pictum'
'Japanese painted fern'

Many gardeners recommend regular sprinkler systems for watering, while some are in the middle of the spectrum. Aldona Satterthwaite, in the Dramatic Garden chapter, recommends replacing a water hungry lawn with low-maintenance perennials. She says that you can train your plants to accept less moisture if you consistently water only once a week, but deeply. Marion Jarvie agrees with deep watering. Her aristocratic garden is a testament to her practice. She advises gardeners to use an amount of water equal to the size of the pot in which the plant came. A one-gallon pot requires one gallon of water once a week, assuming it has not rained all week. She believes that underwatering causes the loss of most plants.

In the Country Garden chapter, Frank Kershaw uses a lot of pea gravel in his garden beds to keep the soil and plants cool and retain moisture on their underside. In her beautiful white garden, Sonia Leslie uses soaker hoses.

It is essential, however, that any new planting be given more frequent watering until it becomes fully established.

There are many options for watering. The choice is yours, but we all need to be aware of the importance of conserving water.

Who is a Master Gardener?

Many of the experts featured in *Gardening from a Hammock* are Master Gardeners who are committed not only to gardening but also to volunteerism within their communities. The designation Master Gardener refers to neither professionals nor amateurs, but rather a hybrid: amateur gardeners, who are well educated, trained and have agreed to help educate the public about gardening.

Master Gardeners of Ontario (MGOI) is a volunteer organization dedicated to providing in-depth, sustainable horticultural information to the public. It began in 1985 as a program of the Ontario Ministry of Agriculture, Food and Rural Affairs but it is now an independent non-profit organization.

The Master Gardener concept was originally created in Washington State (USA) in 1972. Ontario's first pilot sites began in Brigden, Englehart and London with 39 participants. The next year, Brantford, Stratford, Ottawa, Windsor, Algoma West, Burlington and St. Catharines joined and brought with them another 154 new volunteers. By June 2011, there were 540 Master Gardeners and 161 Master Gardeners in Training in 38 chapters in Ontario.

Now, as then, experienced gardeners are recruited locally. After an orientation session, candidates take an eligibility test. If they pass, they may register for on-line courses from either the University of Guelph or The Nova Scotia Agricultural College. Volunteers are Master Gardeners in Training for at least the first two years of membership. During this time they usually complete the educational requirements unless they have previous qualifications.

Participants provide horticultural information to the public via garden advice clinics, workshops, electronic, print and social media, and appearances at public venues. Each volunteer must contribute a minimum of 30 hours of service each year. Because Master Gardeners and Master Gardeners in Training commit to continuously updating their knowledge, they are known for providing reliable information.

For more information, check out
www.mgoi.ca

What is a Low-Maintenance or Easy-Care Plant?

Look for these qualities when you're buying a plant to get the most out of your garden without spending a lot of time caring for it.

An easy-care plant:
- is disease and insect resistant; for example, the plant doesn't suffer from mildew, or, in the case of hostas, doesn't look like Swiss cheese because of slugs
- requires little or no dead-heading
- is relatively drought resistant and doesn't need a lot of watering once it is fully established
- doesn't need any or much fertilizer
- can stay in the same place without needing to be divided too frequently or at all
- requires little or no pruning to keep it looking good
- tolerates heat and humidity and doesn't fade in full sun
- won't invade your garden, unless you want it to fill in a large space where nothing else will grow
- is long blooming for continued colour in the garden
- may naturalize, like daffodils and species tulips, without taking over your garden.

What's in a Name?

Botanical names might sound funny – and it might seem that everyone pronounces them differently – but they are essential in order for you to find the right plant. Nurseries use botanical names rather than a plant's common name because botanical names are standardized whereas one plant can have several common names.

For example, as Belinda Gallagher says "there are 150 different black-eyed Susans; some small, some grow 8-ft tall." To ensure you get the right plant, you need to ask the nursery for the correct botanical name. In the case of the black-eyed Susan we are recommending, you would need to ask for *Rudbeckia fulgida* 'Goldsturm', one of the many black-eyed Susans on the market.

Sources for Plant Names

Wherever possible we have used the latest botanical name for plants, but these can change too, as botanists and plant

Nurseries use botanical names rather than a plant's common name because botanical names are standardized

specialists revise plant families. Our sources for plant names include: Heritage Perennial's the *Perennial Plant Guide* by John Valleau (*www.perennials.com*), the Manual of Woody Landscape Plants by Michael Dirr, and other Internet sources, such as Taunton's Fine Gardening website (*www.finegardening.com*), Connon Nurseries (*www.connon.ca*), Sheridan Nurseries (*www.sheridannurseries.com*), and the Royal Horticultural Society Plant Finder (*apps.rhs.org.uk/rhsplantfinder*).

By all means, continue to use common names – after all one person's Bachelor Button is another's Blue Cornflower – but take the botanical name from our plant chart to the nursery when you go shopping. Or better yet, take this book with you.

A Dramatic Garden

Aldona Satterthwaite is forced to be a lazy gardener. As the former executive director of the Toronto Botanical Garden, if she wanted to work in her garden she had to do it at 5:30 in the morning. Even when she was editor of *Canadian Gardening* magazine, time was a luxury. So when she redesigned her garden six years ago she made it quiet, a place to rest and to play.

However, after 16 years with a shady garden in sandy soil, Aldona moved into a new house with lots of sun. "For years I lied to myself and said my old garden was a sun garden," she admits, which leads to one of her first suggestions for a low-maintenance gardener.

"Deal with reality. Don't pretend to have an English country garden if you have shade."

Like most Master Gardeners, Aldona immediately taps into the need for good soil.

"In order to be a lazy gardener, you first need to be an industrious one. Your initial job is to work on the soil. Go nuts with soil amendment. Add composted manure and tons of compost. Save your leaves in the fall and spread them on the garden and let the worms do the work. If you don't get the soil right, you don't get your garden right. When the soil is healthy and well fed, your plants will be healthier and less prone to disease," she says.

"Some people pooh-pooh watering systems, but they are a boon for the lazy gardener. Make sure the system has a moisture sensor and that you can program it manually. It's far better to water deeply once a week, as more frequent and shallow dribbles only encourage shallow roots and weak plants. You can train your plants to accept less moisture – providing you are consistent."

Aldona doesn't believe in lawns. "Ditch the grass, it takes too much work."

Another way to save a ton of work, advises Aldona, is to group plants with similar needs – even in pots. "If you're time-strapped, limit the amount of containers you have. They require more frequent watering than plants grown in the ground."

Finally, buy healthy, good-quality plants. Look for plants that are bushy, not leggy.

"Simplicity is restful and always beautiful. Gardens with one of everything – that way lies madness," she says.

Aldona recommends colours that make you happy. "Test combinations with annuals before investing in perennials to see if you like the look."

She believes in structure in the garden, choosing backbone plants that pay their way and vines that offer mystery, privacy and a sense of enclosure. She includes shrubs, groundcovers, and broadleaf evergreens, which all serve as a quiet backdrop so she can put anything in front of them.

"I have some old standbys, some of which are inexpensive and popular because they work. I like growing Sarcoxie euonymus

Gillenia trifoliata

Echinacea purpurea 'Vintage Wine'

"Ditch the grass, it takes too much work."

up fences, as over time it creates a living wall and gives you year-round green. You can grow other, more seasonal climbers – such as clematis – over and through it."

Aldona's new garden is in the sun, and she finds that although there were some good plants, there was a lack of drama, substance and stature. "There were loads of pastels, not enough strength of form or colour," she explains. "The garden needed more blues, purples, and dark reds, and maybe shots of white and silvers."

Her sun plants include these:
- Bowman's root (*Gillenia trifoliata*)
- Culver's root (*Veronicastrum virginicum*)
- Beebalm or bergamot (*Monarda* 'Aquarius')
- Crimson scabious (*Knautia macedonica*)
- Autumn stonecrop (*Sedum telephium* 'Matrona')
- Smoke bush (*Cotinus coggygria* 'Royal Purple')
- European beech (*Fagus sylvatica* 'Dawyck Purple')
- Purple coneflower (*Echinacea purpurea* 'Vintage Wine')
- Mountain fleeceflower (*Persicaria amplexicaulis* 'Firetail')
- Eastern blue star (*Amsonia tabernaemontana*)

Bowman's root provides interest in late spring when its airy, white, star-like flowers stay for weeks, then in the fall with its bronze leaves, and finally throughout winter with its lasting seed pods.

New lavender-blue cultivars of **Culver's root,** such as **'Lavender Towers'** or **'Fascination'**, are beefier-looking than older varieties. These grow tall, up to 250 cm, and provide a graceful arch of colour August through September.

The **'Aquarius' beebalm** has incredible magenta-purple flowers, says Aldona, and it is a newer mildew-resistant variety. **Crimson scabious** has deep maroon double pincushion flowers that bloom for weeks in the summer. It is a good filler plant that comes back by self-seeding. It also is excellent for cutting.

The **'Matrona' autumn stonecrop** variety that Aldona suggests echoes the deep reds of the other plants. Continuing with the

❧ *Simplicity is beautiful and always restful.*
❧ *Ditch the lawn; it's too much work.*
❧ *Spread your fall leaves on the garden and let the worms amend your soil.*
❧ *Limit pots as they need lots of watering or use large containers.*
❧ *Test colour combinations with annuals before investing in perennials.*
❧ *Buy plants that are bushy, not leggy.*

- Variegated Japanese Solomon's seal (*Polygonatum odoratum* 'Variegatum')
- Variegated redtwig dogwood (*Cornus alba* 'Elegantissima')
- Maidenhair fern (*Adiantum pedatum*)
- Hellebores (*Helleborus* – any variety)
- Fiveleaf aralia (*Acanthopanax sieboldianus*)

Sarcoxie euonymus is one of Aldona's favourites as it acts as a backdrop to anything; it grows up fences and can create a green living wall over time. Other climbers, such as clematis, can grow over and through the euonymus. In front of it she groups plants like paintings, each one designed to enhance the next, creating more than the sum of its plants.

red and purple colour scheme, Aldona suggests the dramatic **smoke bush** or the columnar, deep purple **European beech**.

The following three plants work well together, adding a colour backbone of reds and blue: hardy **purple coneflower** with

"Solomon's seal is one of those spring plants that make your heart beat faster."

its dark red stems and purple flowers with reddish centres; **fleeceflower** with its deep red flowers; and **eastern blue star** with its willow-like foliage and starry blue flowers.

For the shade garden, Aldona combines a number of plants for different effects. Her shade plant list includes the following:
- Sarcoxie euonymus (*Euonymus fortunei* 'Sarcoxie')
- Golden shadows pagoda dogwood (*Cornus alternifolia* 'Golden Shadows')
- Clematis (*Clematis viticella* 'Betty Corning')
- Yellow barrenwort or bishop's hat (*Epimedium × versicolor* 'Sulphureum')
- Ghost fern (*Athyrium × hybrida* 'Ghost')
- Bowles' golden sedge (*Carex elata* 'Aurea')
- Golden Japanese forest grass (*Hakonechloa macra* 'Aureola')
- Creeping Japanese sedge (*Carex morrowii* 'Ice Dance')
- Lamium (*Lamium maculatum* 'White Nancy')

She designs an illuminating golden portrait of shrubs, perennials, climbers, and grasses that light up in the shade, starting with **'Golden Shadows' pagoda dogwood**. Aldona considers this small tree stunning as its bright yellow-gold variegated leaves brighten up the darkest corner, its horizontal form adds variety, and its white flowers in summer and dark berries in fall make it interesting year-round.

Clematis 'Betty Corning' has lovely, nodding, lavender-blue flowers, says Aldona. "It blooms its socks off for weeks and weeks." The **epimedium** not only forms a lovely carpet of pretty leaves, but the yellow flower works well with **ghost fern** – a hybrid that spreads beautifully – **Bowles' golden sedge**, and **golden Japanese forest grass**. The Japanese forest grass echoes the shape of the sedge, but grows larger. Aldona has these grasses under a soft creamy-yellow-flowered **'Elizabeth' magnolia**, along with an abundance of narcissi.

Aldona fashions another dramatic palate, this time with silver and white. She combines **'Ice Dance' sedge, lamium 'White Nancy'** and variegated **Solomon's**

Monarda 'Aquarius'

seal under an old silver-edged **dogwood**. The leaves of the sedge are trimmed in bright white, while the lamium has silver leaves with white flowers. "Solomon's seal is one of those spring plants that make your heart beat faster," Aldona says about the arching creamy-white-edged leaf whose white drooping flowers signal spring. The dogwood, with its horizontal branches and white-edged leaves, balances the shapes and colours of this corner.

Master Gardener Aldona Satterthwaite is the former executive director of the Toronto Botanical Garden. She has enjoyed a varied and successful writing and editing career. Learn more about the TBG at www.torontobotanicalgarden.ca.

"Simplicity is restful and always beautiful."

For an interesting collection of plants with the same leaf shapes in a variety of sizes, Aldona suggests planting **maidenhair fern** and **hellebores** under **fiveleaf aralia**. These have similar leaf shapes but different textures and sizes.

Epimedium × versicolor 'Sulphureum'

A Sustainable Garden

No Mow! No Blow! No H_2O! is one of the projects Master Gardener Belinda Gallagher introduced at Ontario's Royal Botanical Gardens in Burlington as head of horticulture. The gardens she designed for the project eliminate the need for lawn mowers and leaf blowers and reduce water consumption through intelligent plant selection.

"The minute you plant, there is some kind of maintenance."

Belinda now runs her own horticultural consulting business, Hooked on Horticulture. She also has co-developed and teaches on-line at the University of Guelph's new program, Sustainable Urban Horticulture and Agriculture.

In the spring of 2011, she bought 100 acres of land just south of Algonquin National Park in Central Ontario. About

35 acres include protected wetlands, and Belinda plans to do just that, protect this land, while researching native plants and climate change.

She is passionate about making gardeners more aware of environmental challenges. "I want to be relevant to the greater public in horticulture – be water-wise, reduce our carbon footprint, plant and eat local vegetables. I want to work with young people about environmental issues. The weather is becoming more extreme. We need to be making decisions to respond to that, like drought-tolerant gardening. We need to learn about plants that will work in the future and we have to make sustainable choices."

Belinda also advises that gardeners should know the proper names of plants. "Use botanical names because otherwise you don't know what you are planting. There are 150 different black-eyed Susans; some

TIPS

❖ *Use botanical names to ensure you are buying the right plant.*
❖ *Buy single peonies – their strong stems hold up in the rain and don't require staking.*
❖ *Start small so gardening doesn't become overwhelming.*
❖ *Observe what plants are successful in your neighbours' gardens and try them.*

small, some grow 2.5 metres tall." She suggests observing what the neighbours are growing successfully, doing some homework and using the botanical hotlines. If researching on-line, Belinda recommends Googling reliable sources such as nurseries, horticultural societies and Master Gardener websites.

New gardeners should plant a small garden first so they don't become overwhelmed by the amount of work required even for low-maintenance plants. "The minute you plant, there is some kind of maintenance," she warns.

These plants for the sunny garden bloom sequentially throughout spring summer and fall, with a lot of winter interest. They include:
- Pasque flower (*Pulsatilla vulgaris*)
- Single peony (*Paeonia* 'Flame')
- Meadowrue (*Thalictrum rochebruneanum* 'Lavender Mist')
- Sticky Jerusalem sage (*Phlomis russeliana*)
- Red switch grass (*Panicum virgatum* 'Shenandoah')

Pulsatilla vulgaris

Belinda loves the bright blue blooms of the **pasque flower** but the silky seed heads that follow are even more beautiful. The seed heads also add a longer season of interest. Any **single peony** (as opposed to a double peony) pays for itself in the garden, as these have stems strong enough to hold the giant flowers up and don't require staking. The **'Flame'** cultivar is a

favourite of Belinda's because she likes its bright pink-red colour.

Meadowrue has sprays of lavender-purple above delicate foliage and provides good height in the garden. As a bonus, it attracts bees.

Belinda likes either the yellow or pink forms of **sticky Jerusalem sage** but selected the yellow one because it may be easier to find. It flowers mid-summer over a clump of grey-green foliage. The beauty of the plant, however, is apparent in winter when the snow lands on the mushroom-shaped seed heads, making them look like "cupcakes on a stick." "They have stunning foliage and are very architectural," explains Belinda.

Also very dramatic is the **red switch grass**. "You can't beat them in the fall," says Belinda. They add vertical interest, movement, texture and burgundy colour

"We need to learn about plants that will work in the future and we have to make sustainable choices."

and are easy to care for. She finds them versatile either as a specimen or in a group to create a modern look.

Plants for the shady garden are the following:
- Seven-son flower tree (*Heptacodium miconioides*)
- Solomon's seal (*Polygonatum biflorum*)
- Shieldleaf rodgersia (*Astilboides tabularis*)
- Masterwort (*Astrantia major* 'Ruby Wedding')
- Sweet cicely (*Myrrhis odorata*)

The **seven-son flower tree** is exceptional for its cinnamon peeling bark that provides interest year-round. Belinda describes its foliage as "clean, crisp green that never is eaten by anything." The

Astrantia 'Ruby Wedding'

Phlomis russeliana

Astilboides tabularis

white flowers come out in late summer and fall when there aren't many other flowering shrubs. "The flowers are amazingly fragrant," says Belinda, "and the pink bracts after flowering last into the fall."

"**Solomon's seal** is my favourite plant of all times – today," says Belinda. "It takes dry shade, is very elegant and graceful. I love the flowers but particularly the arching shape of the stems. They emerge like sea serpents from the ground in the spring." She explains that Solomon's seal is usually misnamed in garden centres as the native and non-native (mainly from Asia) are often mixed together. "I like them all. The variegated ones are wonderful but take a longer time to mature and bulk up so people may be disappointed."

Belinda loves the **shieldleaf rodgersia** for its foliage. "The leaves look like they are held aloft. Everyone wants that tropical look and this plant has it. The leaves can be bigger than a large round platter with plumes of white flowers in disc shapes."

Masterwort lasts almost eight weeks in Belinda's garden. "It is a very cool plant because it feels like a dried flower. When picked it lasts a long time in water." The **'Ruby Wedding'** variety is a deeper pink than the species, has pretty foliage and provides colour in the shade in midsummer.

Sweet cicely is a herb known as a natural sweetener. Belinda likes it because of its fragrance, its umbrella shape that attracts pollinators and its cut, furry foliage that stays fresh and green. It self-seeds but not aggressively. She suggests that you combine the airy, fine leaf with a stronger one in the garden, perhaps placing it beside a hosta.

Master Gardener and lecturer, Belinda Gallagher can be reached at Gallagher. belinda@gmail.com, and you can check out her business, Hooked on Horticulture, at www.hookedonhorticulture.com.

The Bold Garden

The catalogues are here, the catalogues are here! These glossy, colourful temptations are the ultimate venue for the lazy gardener. The research is done for us, instructions are clear, and the plants are delivered to our doorsteps. No fighting crowds in May, no impulse buys that don't work and no more losing out for the best picks.

Catalogues shine on dark winter days. Dugald Cameron, former president of *Gardenimport.com*, knows how to create one of the shiniest. *Gardenimport.com* was an Ontario mail-order nursery that specialized in rare, unusual, and high-quality plants. Dugald is famous for his plant choices, his ability to create magical palates, and his generous assistance to gardeners.

For the sunny garden, Dugald chooses bold colours. "Why be boring?" he asks. "People need a little colour. Many people are cursed with foundation plantings,

solid but dull. Colour is uplifting." Dugald is anything but boring. His choices all have a little something special, whether it is a new variety, extra-long blooming habits, double blooms, colourful creepers, or foliage that changes colour from summer to fall.

"I like change in plants," Dugald says. "Plants should be changing all the time. The spring garden is very different than the fall one."

He shares some basic advice: prepare the soil, plant in the right spots, and purchase quality plants from nurseries that are in business all year. "Garden centres need all the business they can get or they will disappear," he explains, and so will all their expertise and plant experimentation.

"Don't give up if you have missed the spring planting season," he says, "because fall is the best time to plant." He explains

Clematis 'Etoile Violette'

Brunnera macrophylla 'King's Ransom'

that plants are usually on sale then and that it is cooler and less stressful on the plants although the soil remains warm. Plants such as peonies, as well as trees and shrubs, actually do best when planted in autumn. Dugald recommends using the lasagna method of preparation in the fall: lay newspapers on the ground where you want a new bed, and pour soil on top of them. Allow time and weather to help rot the newspaper layer, and let the worms work the rotting newspapers and added soil into the ground.

Ultimately, according to Dugald, "you don't know a plant until you grow it. It will be different than you imagine. Remember, it's not a life commitment, and you can buy another. Life is too short. Why keep a plant you don't like?"

His choice of shrubs and perennials for the sunny garden are:

- Bulbs, which include lots and lots of daffodils
- Hybrid musk rose (*Rosa* 'Ballerina')
- Climbing rose (*Rosa* 'Golden Gate')
- Clematis (*Clematis* 'Guernsey Cream')
- Clematis (*Clematis* 'Etoile Violette')
- Clematis (*Clematis* 'Durandii')
- Sweet autumn clematis (*Clematis terniflora*)
- 'Beauty of Moscow' Lilac (*Syringa vulgaris* 'Krasavitsa Moskvy')
- Dwarf lilac (*Syringa* 'Bloomerang')
- Japanese barberry (*Berberis thunbergii* 'Rose Glow')
- Hardy chrysanthemum (*Dendranthema* 'Bolero', 'Samba', and 'Rhumba')
- Blanketflower (*Gaillardia* 'Oranges and Lemons')
- Spike speedwell (*Veronica spicata* 'Red Fox')
- Alpine betony (*Stachys monieri* 'Hummelo')

Dugald is a big fan of bulbs, and for the lazy gardener, they are a must. Bulbs can live in a crowded garden because they don't take up any extra room. They provide some of the first colour and are good companions for later plants, such as daylilies and bleeding heart, because these perennials will hide the dying foliage of the bulbs. He recommends daffodils because squirrels avoid them, there are so many varieties, and many are fragrant.

Dugald also loves roses. "Don't let roses scare you," he says. "There is a mistaken idea that roses are a challenge. They are hardy if you select the right rose. Buy it unpotted since nurseries have to cut the roots to fit roses into pots." Untrimmed roses take less time to become established because they don't suffer from the shock of the root trim. He explains that roses are enduring if they are grown on a hardy rootstock. At the nursery, ask if the root stock is the hardy *Rosa multiflora*, *Rosa laxa*, or *Rosa canina*, which is not as common. Dugald favours the easy-care Kordes landscape roses, which are selected for their abundant bloom, disease resistance and hardiness.

"The **'Ballerina' rose** doesn't look like a rose," says Dugald, "with its sprays of white and pink flowers". These flowers more closely resemble apple blossoms and

"Why be boring? People need a little colour."

bloom almost all summer. The climber **'Golden Gate'** is yellow, a long bloomer and very fragrant.

Dugald recommends planting four different **clematis** to provide bloom throughout the summer. **'Guernsey Cream'** produces creamy-white flowers in June. **'Etoile Violette'** is an older variety of clematis with deep purple flowers that bloom for more than a month in late June. "It's good for beginners because it won't die," says Dugald. "I have never had a garden without one." **'Durandii'** is a favourite because

Syringa vulgaris *'Krasavitsa Moskvy'*-
'Beauty of Moscow' Lilac

Rosa 'Golden Gate'

Dryopteris 'Golden Mist'

it has big denim-blue flowers and blooms all summer. In late summer **sweet autumn clematis** comes out with masses of white, fragrant flowers and covers fences, garages, and whatever stands in its way.

After touring the spectacular lilacs in Hamilton's Royal Botanical Gardens, Dugald was smitten with the **lilac shrub 'Beauty of Moscow'**. Along with its enticing fragrance, this variety has unusual pale, silvery-lilac buds that open in midsummer to double white blooms. These are hardy in most parts of Canada and can be grown any-where with full sun and good drainage. He now adds a **dwarf lilac** to his list of favourites for small gardens, because living up to its name, **'Bloomerang'**, it has a second bloom in midsummer.

If you want people to stop taking short-cuts through your property, Dugald suggests that you plant **Japanese bar-berry**. The thorns keep trespassers away, despite the drawing power of the profuse flowers and the bright red berries, which remain on the plant all winter (unless wildlife snack on them). The foliage of a variegated variety, **'Rose Glow'**, changes from marbled bronze-red and pinkish-white to purple-rose in the fall. This plant thrives in poor, dry soil and can tolerate some shade.

Dugald considers his choices of **chrysan-themum, 'Bolero', 'Samba', and 'Rhum-ba'**, "virtually idiot-proof." They grow into perfect mounds and bloom continually from late summer to frost when most summer perennials fade away. 'Bolero' has deep gold flowers, 'Samba' has rose pink, daisy-like flowers, and 'Rhumba' has deep red buds opening to coral-peach tones.

Blanketflowers are super-tough, perfect for benign neglect in heat and drought. The variety he selects, **'Oranges and Lemons'**, provides a show of up to 75 extra-large, yellow-tipped, soft orange blossoms from midsummer on. If you do a little deadheading, Dugald predicts they will bloom into the fall. This is a prairie native workhorse that thrives in poor, well-drained soil in the baking sun.

The magenta-red spikes of the **spike speedwell** provide sculptural contrast in the garden. It is another foolproof plant,

"If you want people to stop taking shortcuts through your property, plant Japanese barberry."

according to Dugald, and its blooms will last from June throughout the summer in full sun, in poor but well-drained soil, with just a little deadheading.

Dugald can't omit the striking **alpine betony 'Hummelo'** with its spiky pink flowers that bloom up to 40 cm from midsummer to fall.

He cautions that although these choices are hardy and can withstand poor soil and some neglect, we do have to nurture a little, by getting a healthy plant, then by preparing the soil with compost, but chiefly by putting critical effort into watering sufficiently to get the plant established. "Then you can ignore them," he says.

His approach to the shade garden is no dif-ferent, as he couples value with low main-tenance. "My approach is about variety," he explains, "colour and textures you wouldn't see ordinarily, a lot of flower for each precious bit of space. And all the choices are good value for what you will get."

His choices for the shady garden include these:

- Barrenwort or bishop's hat (*Epimedium × perralchicum* 'Frohnleiten')
- Siberian bugloss (*Brunnera macrophylla* 'Looking Glass')
- Soft shield fern (*Polystichum setiferum* 'Herrenhausen')
- Wood fern (*Dryopteris* 'Golden Mist')
- Fern-leaved bleeding heart (*Dicentra* 'Ivory Hearts')
- Dwarf bleeding heart (*Dicentra* 'Burning Hearts')
- Coral bells (*Heuchera* 'Peach Flambé')
- Coral bells (*Heuchera* 'Hercules')
- Serrata hydrangea (*Hydrangea serrata* 'Preziosa')
- Hellebores (*Helleborus × hybridus* 'Ashwood Gold Finch')

Barrenwort is a lazy gardener's treasure in the shade because it will actually grow under just about anything, including maple trees, explains Dugald. This variety, **'Frohnleiten'**, is unusual because while the regular species has blossoms that hide under its leaves, this one holds its delicate butter-yellow blossoms above the heart-shaped leaves so you can see them. The glossy leaves are another bonus: they turn deep red in autumn.

Dugald recommends any variety of **Siberian bugloss** with variegation. He considers **'Looking Glass'** a step above the latest form, 'Jack Frost'. He calls this a very forgiving plant, perfect for busy gardeners. It has heart-shaped leaves that

begin silvery with fine green veins and fade to silver as the season progresses, lighting up the shade like a spotlight. Its sprays of forget-me-not blue flowers in the spring are a bonus. He also recommends **'King's Ransom'** with its silver veins and gold-edged leaves.

Soft shield ferns bring an airy grace, texture, and subtle colour to the garden. Ferns are tough, hardy and work well with most other perennials. Soft shield fern has broad, spreading, light green fronds that are soft to the touch and form delicate, billowing clumps. They become fuller and softer as the plant ages. Dugald encourages the lazy gardener to mix these with hostas. "*Gardening from the Hammock* gardeners will have hostas because they work," he says. He also favours the **wood fern** because it changes from a golden colour in the spring to green by summer, and Dugald embraces change in the garden.

Everyone recognizes bleeding hearts from their granny's garden, but these new varieties require a second look. Smaller than most varieties, **fern-leaved bleeding heart** has white – not red – flowers, on arching stems over blue-green finely cut leaves. The blue leaves look pretty even when this long-flowering dwarf Japanese plant stops blooming. **Dwarf bleeding heart** has red flowers edged with white atop mounds of silvery foliage. The bonus of this cultivar is that it blooms from mid-spring until fall frosts, says Dugald.

What's old is new again and again. **Coral bells** are native plants that have been improved, and now come in brilliant colours of lime green, deep purple, golden-orange, and with much variegation. Dugald's choice is *Heuchera* 'Peach Flambé', as the infusions of red hues and larger, smoother leaves make this plant shine in the shade. "This is an improvement on some other amber-coloured coral bells," he says.

Hydrangea serrata 'Preziosa'

Hydrangeas are favourites because not only do they require minimal care and delight us with snowballs of colour, but if they are not cut down after the frost, they provide winter interest with their dried shapes. The variety **'Preziosa'** is not new, "but it works," says Dugald. A lot of the new hydrangeas are not for the time-pressured gardener as they need too much care. This variety, from the mountains of Japan, is dependable and interesting with deep pink snowball flowers, which deepen to reddish-purple in the fall. Its glossy green leaves take on purple tinges. Gardeners won't have to worry about the soil; if it's more acidic, the blooms will have a bluish cast. 'Preziosa' can grow in either sun or partial shade.

No shade garden would be complete without one of Dugald's favourite plants, **hellebores**. They are all great, he says, and recommends any with × *hybridus* in front of their name, going for any of the brighter ones that show off in the shade. Check out **'Ashwood Gold Finch'** for its glowing, golden-yellow blooms with strawberry-speckled centres. "Hellebores work well under deciduous trees and come in a wide range of colours. They are very long-lived, have attractive foliage all summer, and work well with coral bells."

Dugald Cameron, former owner of Gardenimport Inc., an online and mail-order perennial specialist, can be reached at flower@gardenimport.com.

Berberis thunbergii 'Rose Glow'

A Country-Style, Poetic Garden

"You are creating a composition, a picture with your garden," Frank Kershaw explains. "The geometry and shape of your property is the frame. A garden is a living form of art that changes all the time, a form of art that you are living in, cooking in, and your kids are playing in. It is a form that involves you. The garden of your dreams will change, depending on your needs, lifestyle and available budget."

Frank Kershaw is a teacher – not only because he teaches courses at Toronto's George Brown College and at the Toronto Botanical Garden. Not because he lectures widely or leads garden tours. It's because he can sort and simplify his encyclopaedic knowledge of horticulture, plant history, and garden design with clarity and, dare we say, poetry.

He advises us to first establish the garden outline and define focal points. "What kind of mood do you want to create?" he asks. "In my case, a more natural, organic canopy line of trees defines the outline of my garden. I have a soft, restful, natural country-style garden. "In his garden, focal points or accents include a bright yellow Victorian-style birdhouse, a stone bench, a small pond, rocks with unusual shapes, and two pieces of artwork in the form of cobbled stones forming pictures.

Frank doesn't invite just any plant into his sanctuary. "I choose great plants, but it's harder to select after 40 years," so he has created criteria to help him select exceptional plants. The plants he chose for *Gardening from a Hammock* had to have many of the following characteristics:

- Multi-season interest of foliage, flowers, berries and form.
- Mix of coniferous (evergreens) and deciduous trees. The evergreens give mass and volume for winter interest, create garden walls and provide winter bird habitat.

Pinus aristata

Fothergilla gardenii

- Ability to mature quickly to give full impact without being invasive. "We live in a world where there is a lot of instant gratification, and expectations are heightened. People aren't always prepared to wait seven years for something to bloom."
- Ability to retain colour. Some plants lose their colour intensity with age or too much sun and that can affect their value in plant combinations.
- Narrow upright form. "Many people with smaller residential properties require columnar and dwarf shapes."
- Adaptability to multiple habitats, such as some shade and some sun and dryness.
- Environmental value, such as pollen or larvae source, attractiveness to butterflies. "Butterflies are like flying flowers."
- Ability to create ceilings or walls, to be used as a path edging, to be shaped into topiary or to screen a view.

He also gives us a tip he's used for 27 years to avoid weeding: "I am too busy to weed, so I use a lot of pea gravel as mulch." He scatters these small stones over his sunny rock garden, around the perimeter of his house, and in some of the garden beds. Frank points out that water gets through, but the stones keep the soil and plants cool and retain moisture on their underside, and they block out weeds. He intersperses the pea gravel with larger accent stones to break the monotony and create artistic patterns. In his woodland garden, he uses shredded pine bark mulch. Result? Few weeds.

For the sunny garden, Frank recommends the following:
- Japanese barberry (*Berberis thunbergii* 'Rose Glow')
- Bristlecone pine (*Pinus aristata*)
- Blackberry lily (*Belamcanda chinensis*)
- Crocosmia or montbretia (*Crocosmia* 'Lucifer')
- Tiger flower *(Tigridia)*
- Culver's root (*Veronicastrum virginicum*)
- Chilean oxalis (*Oxalis adenophylla*)
- Prairie smoke (*Geum triflorum*)

The ornamental shrub **Japanese barberry** has a rounded shape with yellow flowers in late spring. Its real beauty is in its new pink growth and deeper maroon foliage in the fall.

The **bristlecone pine** in Frank's front garden has been there 20 years and is only two metres high. "There are some

"A garden is a living form of art that changes all the time."

of these pines thousands of years old and they are still dwarf in their native habitat," explains Frank. The short dark green needles have white resin droplets at the tips providing an accent during winter. As it never needs pruning, it is ideal for the low-maintenance gardener.

Blackberry lily gets its name from the clusters of shiny black seeds exposed when its seed capsules split. Part of the iris family, this lily has sword-shaped leaves that will reach 60 to 90 cm. Its flowers, which appear from July through August, are orange with a red dot and have a spread of five cm.

"**Crocosmia** is the reddest of the reds," says Frank about this tall dramatic plant. In his garden it is an accent against a dark green cedar background, and Frank and his wife enjoy watching the hummingbirds that are attracted to the flame-red flowers in late summer and fall.

Tiger flower also is dramatic, with a variety of bright colours – yellow, red, cream – providing what Frank calls

TIPS

❧ *First establish the garden outline and define focal points.*
❧ *To minimize weeding, use pea gravel as mulch.*
❧ *Mulch keeps soil and plants cool and retains moisture.*
❧ *Evergreens create winter interest, garden walls and winter bird habitat.*
❧ *Choose plants with multi-season interest of foliage, flowers, berries and form.*

incredible blooms. Individual flowers are short-lived but because there are lots of buds, the blooming period lasts several weeks. Frank treats them like annuals because he finds the bulbs turn mushy with the onset of frost.

There's no fuss with **Culver's root**, however. Wand-like white flowers bloom in July and August providing a tall background for other plants. Frank likes the whorled leaves that ring the stem like spokes on an umbrella.

The **Chilean oxalis** is a 15-cm rosy-pink flower with multiple blooms in July through August. What Frank likes is that "it looks like a little pink lipstick tube that opens up." The **prairie smoke** is also great in rockeries and is a native groundcover that acquired its common name from the appearance of its wispy seed heads. "It looks like a pink puff of smoke, with a feathery seed head later in the summer," explains Frank. It blooms from late spring through early summer with clusters of nodding, reddish-pink, maroon, or purple flowers on 30-cm stems. Its deeply cut, fern-like leaves are semi-evergreen; its foliage turns reddish-purple from late fall into winter. It is drought tolerant and spreads, but not invasively.

Frank has an extensive shade garden, and his selections for the shade include the following:
- Fringetree (*Chionanthus virginicus*)
- Chinese witchhazel (*Hamamelis mollis* 'Pallida')
- Dwarf fothergilla (*Fothergilla gardenii*)
- Virginia sweetspire (*Itea virginica* 'Henry's Garnet')
- Leatherwood (*Dirca palustris*)
- Azaleas (especially the Northern Lights series including choices of the following:
- 'Northern Lights' azalea (*Rhododendron* 'Northern Lights')
- 'Lemon Lights' azalea (*Rhododendron* 'Lemon Lights')
- 'Northern Hi-lights' azalea (*Rhododendron* 'Northern Hi-lights')
- 'Rosy Lights' azalea (*Rhododendron* 'Rosy Lights')
- Golden Japanese forest grass (*Hakonechloa macra* 'Aureola')
- Barrenwort or bishop's hat (*Epimedium grandiflorum*)
- Wood poppy (*Stylophorum diphyllum*)
- Maidenhair fern (*Adiantum pedatum*)

The **fringetree** is an unusual small tree, explains Frank, and very slow growing. In his garden, it thrives in light shade. The tree has showy fringe-like flowers that look like "white raindrops" in July. The dark green foliage in summer turns golden-yellow in the fall. The tree has a spreading habit, growing as wide as it is tall.

The **Chinese witchhazel** reminds Frank of rhythmic gymnasts with its yellowish ribbon-like blooms. "It blooms in light to heavy shade, is disease-free for me, tough, and blooms when nothing else is out in early spring," he says.

"If I could have only one shrub, it would be the **fothergilla**, says Frank. "In May, its white flowers look like white bottlebrush cleaners. It looks wonderful with yellow tulips. It has a dense, twiggy, half-arch, even shape which does not require pruning. The dramatic fall foliage turns orange, shades of red and yellow, sometimes on the same plant. It holds its buds throughout the winter. The height is variable – mine are under 90 cm and equally broad."

Crocosmia 'Lucifer'

Frank appreciates **Virginia sweetspire** because it is so adaptable – in full sun or medium shade, it blooms the third week of June when the early shrub flowers are finished and helps transition the garden into summer. The white flowers hang in arches "looking like tails" with white wand-like flowers. The leaves turn reddish-purple in the fall, and Frank's shrub holds its colourful leaves into January.

The **leatherwood** is a slow-growing native shrub almost circular in shape with yellow flowers in early May and a bluish tint to the foliage. What makes this more interesting is that the twigs are very strong and supple and historically have been used for binding, bowstrings and basketry. It can handle deep woodland shade or sun. The only problem may be availability.

The **'Northern Lights' azalea** was developed and released by the University of Minnesota Landscape Arboretum. Any azalea included in this group will have flower-bud hardiness to withstand Minnesota winters. Frank likes this series because there are a variety of colours and size choices, no winter protection is needed in his garden (zone 6) and the plants are adaptable and very hardy. "Other than using mulch, you don't have to do much soil work," he says.

The **golden Japanese forest grass** "is a flashlight in the shade garden that attracts and holds your eye," says Frank. Its bright yellow and green striped leaves highlight its mounding, cascading shape. He uses the grass, which is not invasive and is easy to divide, as a specimen around his pond.

"**Barrenwort** is a wonderful, dependable, no-nonsense groundcover," says Frank. "It takes sun in the rockery and shade in the woodland and keeps its leaves into winter." Frank explains that the groundcover is tough and flexible enough to flourish in dry shade. Depending on the variety, white, pink, or yellowish flowers appear from May to June while the heart-shaped leaves emerge bright green with a slight tinge of pink or red and later turn a deeper green; by autumn they take on yellow to bronze tones.

The **wood poppy** is another beacon of light in the shade garden with its buttery-yellow flowers in May. "They are easy to grow from seed," says Frank, "and they look wonderful with trilliums, which flower at the same time." This native flower has a lightly dissected leaf and, since it is not a big spreader, is easy to control if you want to. But don't confuse this with the invasive, non-native celandine poppy (*Chelidonium majus*), which looks quite similar.

"The Chinese witchhazel reminds me of rhythmic gymnasts with its yellowish ribbon-like blooms."

Finally, "any garden would appreciate a **maidenhair fern**," says Frank. He admires the lacy, doily-like foliage that provides richness to the garden. The fern is 50 cm high and thickens from the root. "It looks delicate, but is tough as nails."

Teacher, lecturer, writer, garden tour leader with more than 30 years working experience in horticulture, Frank Kershaw can be Googled by name for more information.

A Broadleaf and Conifer Garden

Jim Lounsbery has had a love affair for more than 35 years, and the object of his affection continues expanding and blossoming until it dominates his Vineland Nurseries in Beamsville, Ontario. Broadleaf evergreens, you remain the plant of intrigue for this horticulturalist, teacher and speaker.

Jim has kept his hands dirty since graduating in horticulture from Guelph University, throughout his technical research

"Broadleaf evergreens and conifers are definitely considered the backbone of the garden. They come in all shapes, colours and textures, from miniatures to giants, and some change colours."

days at the Horticultural Research Institute of Ontario and while teaching at Niagara College, St. Catharines, and Niagara Parks, Niagara Falls. His experi-

ence includes positions as supervisor of arboretums and the trail system at the Hamilton Royal Botanical Gardens, teacher at the Toronto Botanical Garden and teacher of horticulture at Mohawk College in Hamilton for the past 28 years. All this, while cultivating broadleaf evergreens and conifers at his nursery.

At the risk of Jim's scientific ire, we offer a simplistic explanation to differentiate broadleaf evergreens and conifers: broadleafs have flowers, and conifers don't produce showy ones. The stereotypical broadleaf is a rhododendron or an Oregon holly having "broad leaves," explains Jim, while other broadleaf evergreens may have needle-like leaves. Broadleafs are usually groundcovers or shrubs, he adds.

Broadleafs provide winter interest, texture and colour, and many have lovely spring flowers. As well, many are low maintenance, adapting to either sun or

- Blue holly (male) (*Ilex × meserveae* 'Blue Prince')
- Blue holly (female) (*Ilex × meserveae* 'Blue Princess')
- Barberry cotoneaster (*Cotoneaster dammeri* 'Coral Beauty')
- English ivy (*Hedera helix*)
- Periwinkle (*Vinca minor*)
- Variegated periwinkle (*Vinca minor* 'Illumination')
- Japanese spurge (*Pachysandra terminalis*)
- Euonymus (*Euonymus fortunei* 'Sunspot')
- Euonymus (*Euonymus fortunei* 'Kewensis')

shade, good or poor soil. They are ideal for *Gardening from a Hammock.*

Conifers also are evergreens but most have needles, with the exception of some deciduous forms such as larches. They primarily produce cones, not flowers.

"Broadleaf evergreens and conifers are definitely considered the backbone of the garden. They come in all shapes, colours and textures, from miniatures to giants, and some change colours," Jim says.

Jim chose all broadleaf evergreens and conifers for the low-maintenance garden. These plants are workhorses, providing background, groundcover and filler in sun or shade, poor or excellent soil.

Vinca minor 'Illumination'

Although many of them have been around forever and may not have the cachet of newer perennials, Jim remains besotted. "These plants are tough and easy to maintain, that's why you always come back to them."

Since all the following can take either sun or part to full shade – making them ideal for any garden – Jim has divided his selection into broadleaf evergreens and conifers, rather than any other kind of plants for the sunny or shady garden.

His broadleaf evergreen selection includes the following:
- Boxwood (*Buxus microphylla* 'Green Mound')
- Boxwood (*Buxus microphylla* 'Green Gem')

Ilex × meserveae 'Blue Princess'

Boxwood shrubs are easy to maintain and shear, says Jim. "They provide backbone to the garden, are hardy and readily available. They stand up to abuse and can work with most styles of garden."

The blue holly provides height and texture. You can enjoy it in the fall, and in the winter red berries attract birds. To get the berries, though, you need to plant a male and female plant near one another.

Providing architectural detail, the **barberry cotoneaster** with its multi-stemmed branches creates a shapely and gracefully arching form. It has white flowers in May and coral-red berries in the fall. The **'Coral Beauty'** variety grows taller than most, with a wider spread and large orange-red berries that Jim particularly appreciates. It has dark leaves that turn shades of red and purple in the fall.

The familiar **English ivy** is a great flat groundcover and a rapid spreader, a habit that also can be its downfall, says Jim. There are variegated versions, but they are not as hardy or aggressive as the green versions, he warns. If given the opportunity, ivy also will climb fences, trees or walls, or hang from containers.

Euonymus fortunei 'Sunspot'

Cotoneaster dammeri 'Coral Beauty'

Pachysandra terminalis

"**Periwinkle** is very common, classic, fast growing and tolerates our climate," says Jim. "It is good for shallow and poor soil, and has pretty blue flowers in the spring." There are white or plum-coloured and variegated cultivars available. The **'Illumination'** variety lights up an area with its yellow foliage.

Another hardy groundcover is **Japanese spurge**, which Jim likes because its dark glossy green foliage offers another leaf structure. "You can get the variegated leaf, but it doesn't grow as fast as the straight green species," he explains.

When Jim was doing research, he counted 67 cultivars of **euonymus**. "It's a phenomenal workhorse," he says. "It has the ability to creep or climb up the wall." His selection includes both a large and a small variety. **'Sunspot'**, with its creamy-yellow centre on each leaf, draws the eye into the garden, while the **'Kewensis' euonymus** echoes the leaf shape but boasts tiny leaves, adding texture and interest to the combination.

Conifers that will provide the backbone in the garden include these:
- Icee Blue creeping juniper (*Juniperus horizontalis* 'Monber')
- Hinoki false cypress (*Chamaecyparis obtusa* 'Nana Lutea')
- Norway spruce (*Picea abies* 'Little Gem')
- Japanese pyramidal yew (*Taxus cuspidata* 'Capitata')

The **Icee Blue creeping juniper** is a newer cultivar with silver-blue needles that turn purple-pink in the winter. It is the only plant listed above that needs full sun.

"Boxwood shrubs stand up to abuse and can work with most styles of garden."

Jim likes the tougher yellow forms of the **Hinoki false cypress** for the low-maintenance gardener. In his catalogue, he refers to the **'Nana Lutea'** as a lemon golden dwarf. It has a dark green leaf with a yellow edge that darkens in the winter, he explains.

The rounded dwarf **Norway spruce** looks good in a triangular grouping or alone, says Jim, and is ideal in smaller gardens. The **yews** provide contrast with their simple conical shape. "Shear them to the size you want, and they will serve as hedges, backdrops, borders or part of a grouping."

Jim Lounsbery's Vineland Nurseries specializes in dwarf and unusual evergreens, Japanese maples, bamboos, rhododendrons and heathers. He can be reached at jlounsbe@vaxxine.com or www.vinelandnurseries.com .

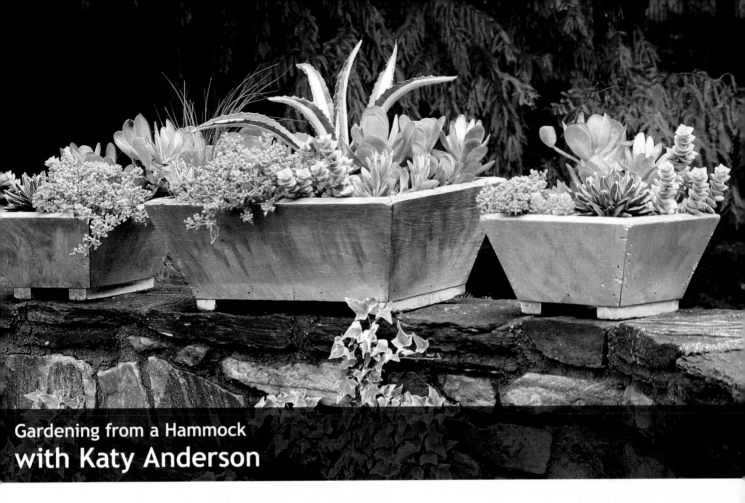

A Trough Garden

Katy Anderson wasn't always an adventurous, forward-thinking Master Gardener. In fact, when she was a high school teacher, raising two children, she went to several meetings of the Ontario Rock Garden Society (now the Ontario Rock Garden and Hardy Plant Society) and decided not to renew her membership. "I didn't understand a thing they were saying," she admits. Happily, she returned and eventually became president of the society and then treasurer of the Toronto Master Gardeners.

"Take things a little piece at a time," she advises novice gardeners. Her advice is perfect for the time-challenged gardener: "If I get to it, I get to it. If I don't, it's not the end of the world. I am not a fussy gardener; I don't have a *Homes and Garden* garden."

What she does have is a cottage, which causes her to focus primarily on spring and fall plantings in her city garden. In addition, Katy has incorporated her love of troughs into her garden, the ultimate lazy gardener's dream. "Once you have a trough, fill it with a gravelly mixture, a few rocks and alpines, and there's nothing else you have to do. In the winter just cover it with some evergreen branches."

A trough is an interesting way to display small flowers as it mirrors a tiny garden. Katy explains that initially people started using water troughs from farms, but now troughs are made from a variety of materials. The best known is tufa – a by-product of volcanic eruption, not unlike pumice. There also are many concrete troughs. They typically are filled with a gravel mixture and a few rocks, and then planted with hardy, drought-resistant alpine, rock and dwarf plants.

"They are fabulous for small gardens and sunny balconies," Katy says. As well,

TIPS

- Take things a little piece at a time.
- Trough gardens are ideal for the lazy gardener with less bending, weeding and watering.
- If you have a cottage or travel in the summer, focus your city garden on spring and fall plantings.

- Bird's-eye primrose (*Primula laurentiana* 'Fernald')
- Prickly saxifrage (*Saxifraga tricuspidata*)
- Creeping thyme, mother-of-thyme (*Thymus serpyllum* 'Pink Chintz')
- Canadian hemlock (*Tsuga canadensis* 'Curly')

Katy suggests planting in small groupings and, in the chart below indicates the position of each plant within the trough.

The **rock cress** is a gentle creeper that grows to about six cm with mounds of deep green hairy foliage that is covered in spring with pretty violet flowers. The

troughs come in all sizes and weights. They can be placed off the ground on tables, chairs and stands and are ideal for an aging population who can tend them without bending over or for those in wheelchairs to enjoy.

Katy has several troughs in her backyard and a giant show-stopper in the front that she planted seven years ago and has moved many times. Crown rot is often the death of plants in troughs, but one way to prevent it is to plant so the crown of the plant is above the gravel, not sitting in it. When choosing the plant combinations for a trough, Katy always includes at least two dwarf evergreens and one plant that drapes over the side of the trough. Plants that do well in troughs need at least four to five hours of sun.

Thymus serpyllum 'Pink Chintz'

The following combination of alpine and rock garden plants is one of Katy's favourite trough plantings and is a good beginning for *Gardening from a Hammock*. The textures, forms and colours complement one another for interest year-round.

- Rock cress (*Aubrieta pinardii*)
- Alpine columbine (*Aquilegia discolor*)
- Alpine pink (*Dianthus alpinus*)
- White whitlow grass (*Draba norvegica*)
- Whitlow grass (*Draba rigida* var. *bryoides*)
- Edelweiss (*Leontopodium alpinum*)

Tricyrtis hirta

"Troughs are ideal for an aging population who can tend them without bending over."

columbine is only about two cm larger and has soft blue and creamy-white nodding flowers. The **alpine pink carnations** mimic the more common ones with clumps of green leaves and large single pink flowers, but they are much smaller and more delicate.

Imagine a low evergreen mat of tiny white flowers in early spring and you can envision the **white whitlow grass.** The other variety of this grass has yellow flowers above dark green minute leaves.

Edelweiss is not just a pretty song, but another alpine plant that in late spring blooms with white flowers over silver-grey foliage. One of the taller flowers is the **primrose** – it blooms in lilac colours on a stalk that grows 10 to 40 cm high. The **prickly saxifrage** is considered a sub-shrub. It has reddish-tinged stems with leathery leaves and pale yellow flowers with bright yellow centres on erect reddish stems. The popular **creeping thyme** provides a carpet of leaves anywhere and produces a mat of bright green leaves with clusters of pink flowers in the trough.

Katy's favourite is the **Canadian hemlock** because it rises and branches out horizontally, adding yet another dimension to the trough.

Thinking outside the trough, Katy has a myriad of shade plants to recommend. This list of shady plants includes a small portion of Katy's favourites:

- Hellebore (*Helleborus × hybridus* 'Eco Dragon's Blood')
- Hellebore (*Helleborus × hybridus* 'Maroon')
- Hellebore (*Helleborus × hybridus* 'Pink Veined' or 'Pink Stripe')
- Welsh poppy (*Meconopsis cambrica*)
- Paperbark maple (*Acer griseum*)
- Witchhazel (*Hamamelis × intermedia* 'Arnold Promise')
- Dwarf European larch (*Larix decidua* 'Little Bogle')

Plant placement for the trough

Rock cress (*Aubrieta pinardii*)	6 cm	Front left corner
Alpine columbine (*Aquilegia discolor*)	8 cm	Centre left
Alpine pink (*Dianthus alpinus*)	5–10 cm	Back left corner
White whitlow grass (*Draba norvegica*)	10 cm	Front right corner
Whitlow grass (*Draba rigida* var. *bryoides*)	5 cm	2 plants, back and centre
Edelweiss (*Leontopodium alpinum*)	15–20 cm	Where it fits
Bird's-eye primrose (*Primula laurentiana* 'Fernald')	10 cm	Inside left corner
Prickly saxifrage (*Saxifraga tricuspidata*)	15–25 cm	To left of the hemlock in the back right corner
Creeping thyme, mother-of-thyme (*Thymus serpyllum* 'Pink Chintz')	5 cm	Front right corner
Canadian hemlock (*Tsuga canadensis* 'Curly')	10 cm tall; lateral branches spread to 30 cm	Back right corner

- Gold cypress (*Chamaecyparis obtusa* 'Fernspray Gold')
- Toad lily (*Tricyrtis hirta*)
- Dwarf astilbe (*Astilbe × crispa* 'Lilliput')
- Coral bells (*Heuchera* 'Georgia Peach' and 'Crispy-Curly')

Katy homes in immediately on **hellebores** to begin the show in the shade. They bloom early in the spring and provide colour until the heat dries up the cup-shaped thick and waxy leaves in midsummer. "Perfect for *Gardening from a Hammock*," says Katy. "Put them in and do nothing except in early spring cut off the dead leaves from last year. It takes about two and a half minutes for each plant." The **'Eco Dragon's Blood'** cultivar is one she has had for years and "loves with a passion." She bought the *Helleborus × hybridus* **'Maroon'** as a plug, moved it twice, and it is thriving. Other varieties provide different colours and Katy recommends any and all.

The **Welsh poppy** is a favourite because its small orange blooms last from spring until frost. It self-seeds but is easy to remove.

For shape in the garden, Katy suggests a small maple and several shrubs. The **paperbark maple** is dramatic with its exfoliating bark in the winter and its upright architectural detail. It can be planted in full sun to part shade. The vase-shaped **'Arnold Promise' witchhazel** is as tall as it is wide, with outward growing branches that bring much-needed colour, as well as fragrance, from February through March. Katy explains that it can be trimmed back and formed into a small tree or bush by pruning once a year after it blooms. Although the books say this shrub needs full sun, Katy has hers in semi-shade.

The **gold cypress** also can handle half shade as well as full sun, says Katy. She admires the golden tips on this evergreen.

Despite its unfortunate name, Katy favours the **toad lily** for its white and purple colour in late fall when the family has returned from the cottage. These

"Georgia Peach has enough glow to catch your eye even without its white sprays of flowers."

funnel-shaped violet spotted flowers have purple centres. Also waiting for her return from the cottage are the **dwarf astilbes**, with their pink flowers swaying above ferny green foliage. Despite their delicate shapes, these are hardy plants and Katy also has several at her cottage.

No shade garden would be complete without **coral bells**, now available in a

wide assortment of colours and textures. The ones Katy favours provide great impact for their size. **'Georgia Peach'** has huge peach-coloured leaves and a large lush habit. Foliage colour changes from peach-orange tones in the spring to rose-purple in the fall.

'Georgia Peach' has enough glow to catch your eye even without its white sprays of flowers.

Master Gardener Katy Anderson is the former president of the Ontario Rock Garden and Hardy Plant Society. To find out more about plants for troughs and rock gardens, contact www.onrockgarden.com.

Heuchera 'Georgia Peach'

A Small, Urban Garden in Purple, Yellow and Cream

"In a small garden, people should not shy away from big gestures. Bold, oversized elements contrast nicely with delicate plants," says landscape designer Kim Price. She is up to the challenge of designing a low-maintenance garden in the city.

Her company, Kim Price Landscape Design, based in the Beaches area of Toronto, has won several awards for small urban gardens. Her overriding philosophy is that a garden is to enjoy. And to have that, you work on getting the form and design to flow. Form and design bring together hard elements such as paving stones and wood and soft elements such as plants, including grass.

"I think a garden should feel unified and work as a whole instead of unrelated bits," says Kim. "To do that, stay with one or two types of stone, select a few main plants and repeat them, and have a couple of colours throughout the garden. Keep consistent; don't wander from Japanese to modern to wild English styles.

"It's really important to figure out exactly where seating should be and how it relates to your house. Establish the bones of the garden, the pathways, terrace and retaining walls.

"Paths are important. They offer movement in the garden. If you do have a path, it's good to not always see the end of it, so it adds depth and mystery and leads you to journey through. Or place something at the end of a path that beckons you, like a bench.

"The famous English landscaper John Brookes uses simple geometric shapes, such as rectangles with circles. You think

TIPS

❀ *Use simple geometric shapes for your design.*

❀ *Consider one primary and two less dominant colours for the garden.*

❀ *Select a few main plants and repeat them to maintain the flow of the design.*

❀ *Place something interesting at the end of a path.*

❀ *Don't be a perfectionist.*

- Paperbark maple tree (*Acer griseum*)
- European beech tree (*Fagus sylvatica* 'Dawyck Purple')
- Seven-son flower tree (*Heptacodium miconioides*)
- Dwarf Serbian spruce (*Picea omorika* 'Nana')
- Golden dwarf threadleaf false cypress (*Chamaecyparis pisifera* 'Filifera Aurea Nana')
- Dwarf fountain grass (*Pennisetum alopecuroides* 'Hamelin')
- Siberian iris – any blue or purple variety (*Iris sibirica*)
- Salvia (*Salvia × sylvestris* 'May Night')
- Tickseed (*Coreopsis verticillata* 'Moonbeam')
- Black-eyed Susan (*Rudbeckia fulgida* 'Goldsturm')
- Speedwell (*Veronica* 'Sunny Border Blue')
- Chameleon spurge (*Euphorbia dulcis* 'Chameleon')

you are being boring but keeping things simple ends up looking better. Keep the framework simple and focus on the plants.

"Consider different textures and sizes of plants. Play with your garden. Instead of laying out your plants from small to larger, have some large grass at the front that you can see through, something unexpected. One that is airy and misty is red switch grass (*Panicum virgatum*).

"Think of colour. Multi-colours won't be as relaxing as one prevailing colour and two less dominant. For example, imagine purple as the main colour – more than half of the garden – with a butter-yellow and cream as secondary colours. Sometime the design dynamic comes from the power of opposites: the old and the new; the rustic and the fine. Think of the refinement of a boxwood hedge and behind it poppies or anemones."

To help simplify the myriad of choices for the low maintenance gardener, Kim eventually decides to keep a soft yellow, blue and purple colour theme for both the sunny and shady garden, although for the shady garden her choices of perennial plants reinforce her emphasis on foliage and texture rather than blooms.

Her choices for the sunny garden include these:

"I love trees, and plant lots of them, even in small spaces."

It takes some discussion to narrow the selection of trees. "I love trees, and plant lots of them, even in small spaces." Kim eventually selects the **paperbark maple,** which climbs five to seven metres but is slow growing and is a less common variety than normally seen in southern Ontario neighbourhoods. Kim loves its cinnamon-red bark that peels like birch. Its green leaves turn a bright red-orange in the fall, providing dynamic colour. Another advantage is that it is insect-resistant.

Kim adores all beech trees, but the **'Dawyck Purple' European beech** is special with its dark purple leaves and columnar shape. "Beeches are fabulous for hedges," says Kim, "because the leaves turn a bronzy colour in the fall and may stay on during the winter."

Salvia × sylvestris 'May Night'

Ligularia 'Little Rocket'

Rudbeckia fulgida 'Goldsturm'

Carex morrowii 'Ice Dance'

Seven-son flower tree is an unusual flowering type because its main feature is its seed clusters. These emerge light green and ripen into a purple colour that remains for many weeks. Flowers are abundant, small and creamy-white. They bloom from mid-August to late September.

"Dwarf spruces are not used often enough," says Kim, praising the **dwarf Serbian spruce 'Nana'** for its glossy blue-green foliage with white bands on the underside of the needles. She likes its pyramidal shape and the fact that this dwarf plant is slow-growing and doesn't need much pruning. She recommends using it on either side of a walkway to an entrance or in three different spots throughout the garden as a repeat of evergreen.

Next she selects **golden dwarf threadleaf false cypress 'Filifera Aurea Nana'**, which grows roughly one metre high. This variety – and there are many so be wary – is a mounding weeping plant with golden thread-like branches that lend a graceful texture.

Kim chooses a grass to provide textural contrast. **Dwarf fountain grass 'Hamelin'** has dark green blades that resemble water flowing from a fountain. This plant produces beautiful arching foliage and flower spikes in late August, explains Kim.

Perennials are the lazy gardener's best friends, provided we find the right ones. Kim recommends ones that are long-blooming with foliage that stays attractive until frost.

In keeping with the colour scheme, she suggests any blue or purple variety of **Siberian iris** to provide blooms from May through June. Following that, add **salvia 'May Night'**, which will provide indigo-blue flowers in late June through July. This plant also draws butterflies and bees with its fragrant leaves and long, cigar-shaped flower clusters.

The reliable **'Moonbeam' tickseed** picks up from there with buttery-yellow colour from June through September, while the **'Goldsturm' black-eyed Susan** provides golden flowers from August through October.

The **'Sunny Border Blue' speedwell** has navy-blue spiked flowers blooming from summer through fall and is very dramatic if mass planted. It stands erect and can withstand dry conditions.

The **chameleon spurge** won the award of merit at the Chelsea Flower Show, says Kim, and for good reason. Plants form a mound of stunning burgundy-purple foliage, bearing small clusters of greenish-yellow flowers, flushed with purple in spring and early summer. "It works magic against contrasting golden foliage."

"Plants in a small garden need to earn their keep."

Kim believes that plants in a small garden need to earn their keep, and she knows which ones do just that. "In dealing with shade, you don't often get a lot of bloom, so I like to deal with form, leaf shape, leaf colour, sizes and textures."

Her suggestions for a shady garden include these:
- Serviceberry (*Amelanchier* x *grandiflora* 'Autumn Brilliance')
- Boxwood (*Buxus microphylla* 'Green Gem')
- Dwarf Canadian hemlock (*Tsuga canadensis* 'Jeddeloh')
- Creeping Japanese sedge (*Carex morrowii* 'Ice Dance')
- Coral bells (*Heuchera* 'Plum Pudding')

Hosta 'Great Expectations'

- Ligularia (*Ligularia* 'Little Rocket' and *Ligularia dentata* 'Desdemona')
- Hosta (*Hosta* 'Great Expectations')
- Foamflower (*Tiarella* 'Iron Butterfly')
- Barrenwort or bishop's hat (*Epimedium × perralchicum* 'Frohnleiten')
- Red barrenwort or bishop's hat (*Epimedium × rubrum*)
- Leatherleaf spurge (*Euphorbia amygdaloides* var. *robbiae*)

The native **serviceberry tree** is one of her favourites as it provides beauty year-round. "I love it because it has beautiful white blossoms in May, edible berries and scarlet leaf colour in the fall," she says.

Kim decided on **boxwood** as a hardy evergreen shrub, specifically the variety **'Green Gem'** as it is slow-growing, which bodes well for lazy gardeners since it requires less trimming and shaping. She points out that this shrub is a broad-leaf evergreen without sharp needle foliage. "Boxwoods grow in total shade and total sun. You can prune them to any size you want. Or you can just leave them. They are an ideal low-maintenance evergreen for the *Gardening from a Hammock* gardener."

Dwarf hemlocks are another favourite because they are slow-growing (they reach 1.5 m but it takes 16 years) and graceful in their cascading form. They grow in shade or sun and are especially lovely cascading over a water feature, suggests Kim.

Her choice of an ornamental grass, **creeping Japanese sedge 'Ice Dance'**, handles half sun or shade and flowers from June to July. The variegated green and cream leaves provide interest throughout the season. The **coral bells 'Plum Pudding'** have deep purple leaves that reinforce the colour scheme.

The two varieties of **ligularia** complement one another. **'Little Rocket'** produces tall spikes of bright yellow flowers in midsummer, with some of the flower spikes 30 cm tall on the existing 90 cm plant. The **'Desdemona'** variety has purple colour on the underside of its leaf. Kim prefers them as focal point plants because their leaves are large and the rocket flower spikes catch the eye.

The large **hosta** ties in with the blue, purple and yellow colour scheme as **'Great Expectations'** has a variegated blue-gold leaf. Kim highly recommends the deeply cut green and purple leaves of the **foamflower 'Iron Butterfly'** to work with the hosta.

She favours **barrenwort** because it grows almost anywhere, including under maple trees. The barrenwort produces buttery-yellow (**'Frohnleiten'**) and crimson (*rubrum*) flowers in spring and is evergreen and vigorous. The **leatherleaf spurge** is hardy, reliable and a slow-spreading groundcover with tiny yellow flowers in late spring.

Kim understands that some of us want an instant show. If that is the case, she recommends buying larger, more mature plants but cautions that they will need to be especially well watered their first couple of seasons.

She has more advice for the non-gardening gardener: "Don't be a perfectionist. Ignore some weeds and the slugs in the hostas. Enjoy your garden. Relaxation is not only a physical state, but a mental one as well."

Master Gardener Kim Price, award-winning designer of Kim Price Landscape Design Inc., specializes in the urban garden. You can reach her at kimpricelandscapedesign.com.

The Experimental Garden

Lindsay Dale-Harris loves to make mistakes. She experiments. She doesn't mind trying things that might not work. Like the lilac garden – "Some things never hang together terribly well" – or the meadow garden– "Once upon a time I took out grass, put seeds down and watched it grow. It looks good certain times of the year, dreadful at others."

Yet last winter after taking a course about vegetable gardens, Lindsay created a series of raised beds. "We put in boxes, made tepees, placed gravel around boxes and planted for colour, design and depth. It was magnificent with exceptions: it was too wet for tomatoes and the kale attracted bugs which ate the broad beans." The experiment growing cucumber in a gravel garden? Worked great.

"A failure is an opportunity to try something new again," explains Lindsay.

As a mother of five and with a busy practice as a town planner, Lindsay joined the Civic Garden Centre (now the Toronto Botanical Garden) for interest. When her children got older, she completed the two-year Master Gardener program from the University of Guelph in 1999. Lindsay has served in many capacities at the Toronto Botanical Garden, including a stint as president and chair of the capital campaign for renovation.

She has two gardens, one in downtown Toronto and the "real" garden on her 200-acre farm north of the city. She keeps the city garden simple, in deference to her two dogs who "race around the garden, ripping things up." Her home garden includes boxwood, pachysandra, rhododendrons and hydrangeas in the front. In the backyard, she has planted boxwood, white roses and geraniums. "I have the perfect hammock garden," Lindsay

❧ *Don't be afraid to experiment – a failure is an opportunity to try something new again.*

❧ *Bulbs are ideal for the lazy gardener.*

❧ *Plant daffodils with hostas to hide the fading daffodil foliage.*

- Peony – any
- Daphne (*Daphne mezereum* var. *rubra*)
- Fireworks goldenrod (*Solidago rugosa* 'Fireworks')
- Aster (*Aster* 'Little Carlow')
- Zinnias, dahlias
- Species tulips – any and all kinds

explains. "I don't have to do anything but clip boxwood. And not that often."

The family's farm is a different story. As Lindsay puts it, "over the years different things happened," including taking the advice of a famous visiting Irish garden designer, Helen Dillon, who informed Lindsay that the garden was "all wrong." Lindsay rushed to take her advice. "We should have had plans but we just raced ahead."

"A garden failure is an opportunity to try something new again."

"What I like best is having lots of opportunities to experiment although not every bit is successful. We have no master plan."

Learning from mistakes is the best teacher, and Lindsay makes it easy for the lazy gardener by sharing from her vast knowledge and experience.

"For me, my garden is lovely because I work in it, but it's not a showpiece," she warns.

She offers the following recommendations for hardy plants that require minimum maintenance in a sunny garden:
- Black Beauty elder (*Sambucus nigra* 'Gerda')
- Sutherland Gold elder (*Sambucus racemosa* 'Sutherland Gold')
- False cypress (*Chamaecyparis*)
- Dwarf goat's beard (*Aruncus aethusifolius*)

Lindsay favours the **elderberry shrubs** for their colour and winter interest. The leaves of the **Black Beauty** are such a dark purple that they appear black. The pink buds grow larger throughout the spring, and by June they open into clusters of pink starflowers. The blossoms have a lemon fragrance. Berries attract birds in the fall. This plant is very sturdy and can get tall and rangy if it isn't cut back. "The good news," says Lindsay, "is that you can hack away to get whatever shape you like without worrying about killing the shrub." The **Sutherland Gold** has golden foliage all season and creamy-white flowers in the spring, followed by red berries. Its relatively fine texture sets it apart from other shrubs.

False cypress has a soft look and nice colour, says Lindsay, but the best part is that you don't need to do anything for or to them.

Dwarf goat's beard provides tall, arching, creamy-white blooms in mid-summer on delicate, fern-like foliage. These plants look good under tall trees, adding colour in darker corners. They require little maintenance.

She is fond of **peonies** "because you don't need to worry about them." They provide giant blooms, and many varieties bloom from spring to later in the summer. "I have taken peonies from other gardens and they have flourished. Modern single-flower peonies don't flop over in the rain as much as the double-flower ones."

Lindsay favours the fragrant **daphne shrub** for its compact form and non-

Sambucus racemosa 'Sutherland Gold'

Hosta 'June'

Aruncus aethusifolius

invasive character. She considers it an easy-growing plant for a small city garden. "In fall I like **goldenrod**," says Lindsay, "in particular **'Fireworks'** as it starts small and has long plumes of bright yellow blooms that provide good colour mid-September."

The **blue aster 'Little Carlow'** grows only 90 cm tall, has a true blue colour and spreads nicely, unlike other varieties that sometimes can grow tall and spindly.

Bulbs are ideal for the lazy gardener, and Lindsay plants about 800 each year on her farm – clearly she's a big fan. One year she experimented by planting daffodils in a giant diamond shape that she can view from her upper window. Another year she planted white daffodils to look like a white flowing river.

Her favourite bulbs include **species tulips**. Species or botanical tulips require minimal care, increase slowly and are less susceptible to pests and disease than are other tulips. Different species bloom from early spring to early summer. She recommends planting the species tulips for naturalizing as she finds that they don't peter out after a few years like the hybrid ones.

She fills in with annuals such as **zinnias** and **dahlias.** Both these annuals come in a variety of forms, sizes and brilliant colours. Zinnias may re-seed every year as well.

For the shady garden, hostas are the natural choice for lazy gardeners, according to Lindsay. "My garden is big and I need substance. These help."

She chooses them plus several viburnums and a number of other plants that are happy in the shade, such as these:
- Dogwood 'Golden Shadows' (*Cornus alternifolia*)

- Arctic Fire red osier dogwood (*Cornus sericea* 'Farrow')
- Oak-leaved hydrangea (*Hydrangea quercifolia*)
- Fragrant snowball (*Viburnum carlcephalum*)
- Dwarf fragrant viburnum (*Viburnum farreri* 'Nanum')
- Doublefile viburnum (*Viburnum plicatum f. tomentosum* 'Mariesii')
- Hosta (*Hosta* 'Niagara Falls')
- Hosta (*Hosta* 'Paul's Glory')
- Hosta (*Hosta* 'June')
- Hosta (*Hosta* 'Sum and Substance')
- Hosta (*Hosta* 'Fire and Ice')
- Dwarf cranesbill (*Geranium* × *cantabrigiense* 'Biokovo' and *Geranium* × *cantabrigiense* 'Cambridge')

Variegated dogwood 'Golden Shadows' is outstanding, says Lindsay. It has the classic layered habit of the dogwood, but its leaves with their broad gold edge on the lime-green background make this cultivar special. It contrasts wonderfully with the **Arctic Fire red osier dogwood**. This dogwood is more compact, about 120 centimetres tall, and has tiny white flowers that turn into clusters of white fruit. However, it is the bright red winter stems against the white snow that makes this shrub a favourite.

She thinks hydrangeas are wonderful because they grow tall, have nice flowers and thrive in the shade. The **oak-leaved hydrangea** in particular is interesting because the leaves are the shape of the red oak leaf and turn a wine colour in autumn. The bark on older branches exfoliates in thin patches.

Lindsay can't get enough **viburnums,** selecting cultivars that range from tiny to very large. She emphasizes that they do well in the fall, and are beautifully fragrant.

Fragrant snowball is open and loose, says Lindsay, with white scented blooms in

Hydrangea quercifolia

late spring. The **dwarf fragrant viburnum** has a tidy small rounded form and is extremely perfumed. Its flowers turn from pink to white as they mature. It has one of the earliest spring blooms and is very fragrant. "It's a choice shrub. It comes out early and it's splendid," emphasizes Lindsay. In contrast, Lindsay says she "hacks away" at her **doublefile viburnum,** which can grow up to four metres tall. The doublefile viburnum is noted for its distinctively layered horizontal branching and the profusion of white lace-cap clusters of blooms on the branches in early spring. Flower clusters appear in two rows, accounting for the name. The dark green leaves turn reddish-purple in fall.

Despite her love of viburnum, Lindsay identifies **hostas** as the ultimate plant for the lazy gardener. She emphasizes that "the absolute lowest maintenance plant is the hosta."

Choosing from the hundreds of sizes, colours and textures is a job for a pro, and

"For me, my garden is lovely because I work in it."

Lindsay obliges. She has experimented with many hostas and has one warning: "In spring, hostas are an ugly mess so plant dwarf daffodils that pop up and cover the hosta stems then die away when the hosta leaves open. Hostas with great big strong leaves are more slug resistant," says Lindsay. **Hosta 'Niagara Falls'** is a good example. It has dark grey-green pointy leaves with a waxy sheen and heavy corrugation. Its pale violet flowers emerge in July.

Hosta 'Paul's Glory' has bright yellow leaves with a wide blue-green margin. Near-white flowers appear in July. **Hosta 'June'** has golden leaves bordered by blue and green. **'Sum and Substance'** does add substance to the garden with its huge chartreuse-yellow leaves and quilted

texture. Pale purple flowers appear in July. **'Fire and Ice'** is variegated with a large white centre and very dark green margins on pointy leaves.

To add colour to the shady garden's foliage, once the viburnum have bloomed, Lindsay plants lots of perennial **geraniums**. "Any geraniums are great as groundcovers." She recommends planting them in large clumps to make a statement.

As well as the popular 'Rozanne' geranium, which flowers continually, **geranium 'Biokovo'** is a favourite because it is very fragrant. These plants form a low spreading mat of fragrant dark green evergreen leaves with clusters of white flowers and a tinge of soft pink. They have a long flowering season from late spring to late summer. **Geranium 'Cambridge'** also is fragrant and forms a groundcover of evergreen leaves, but this cultivar has bright magenta-pink flowers that lighten up the shade. "This is a tough, resilient groundcover," adds Lindsay, recommending that you underplant it in the spring with bulbs. A baby-pink three-centimetre flower emerges above green foliage in May. Leaves turn red in the fall. "Plant the geraniums in clumps," is her final word on geraniums.

Master Gardener Lindsay Dale-Harris is former President of the Toronto Botanical Garden, past Chair of its Capital Fundraising Campaign and sits on its finance committee. She also volunteers to organize out-of-town tours for the TBG.

A "Onesy-Twosy" Garden

Lorraine Flanigan is the furthest thing from a lazy gardener you can imagine. She's a self-proclaimed "onesy-twosy" gardener, with a large number of diverse and experimental plants in her yard.

Her garden is her lab. "Plant growers send me one or two of their new cultivars in the hopes that I will love them and write about them. I love the fact that my garden is high maintenance." However, Lorraine knows that espaliering a magnolia tree or a 'Black Lace' sambucus is not for everyone.

As a Master Gardener, former garden magazine editor and freelance garden writer, she not only writes articles for national gardening publications but also has started some serious garden blogging. "It's a creative outlet and a way of talking to a community," she explains. She follows about 30 other blogs as well, and her garden reflects her involvement with a large gardening community. As well, Lorraine is editor of Trellis, the magazine of the Toronto Botanical Garden.

Like all experts, she begins with soil preparation. She tells the story of a well-known landscaper, Lyndon Miller, who transforms parks in New York City. The soil in one park was impenetrable, heavily compacted, oddly enough, by thousands of pigeon feet. She put a deep layer – about 15 cm – of compost on top, and by the end of the season the worms had moved the compost into the dense soil, creating a fertile environment.

"Let the soil feed your plants so you don't have to," says Lorraine.

She suggests choosing plants for their colourful foliage and has a personal preference for chartreuse, that bright lime-green colour that brightens an area. "Anything with chartreuse has a punch to it," she says.

TIPS

❧ *Take the time to improve the soil – your plants will reward you with health and vigour.*

❧ *Keep weeds in check by mulching beds year-round.*

❧ *Easy to grow, self-seeding forget-me-nots make an impressive display with spring bulbs.*

❧ *Flowers are fleeting; foliage is forever. Choose perennials with colourful leaves for season long interest.*

The dramatic **Russian sage** provides impact with its airy foliage and blue flowers. It blooms from late summer into fall and is very drought tolerant. **'Filigran'** features even lacier and more finely cut foliage than the more common variety.

To be clear, **'Shortwood' phlox** is not short but is named after a garden writer with that name. Its vigorous pink flowers last about three weeks midsummer to early fall, attracting butterflies and hummingbirds.

Use plants that self-seed, Lorraine advises, listing Shirley poppies and Brazilian verbena as great self-seeders for the sun, and forget-me-nots and lady's mantle for the shade. "Let seeds do the work for you."

Lorraine couldn't be dissuaded from including **geranium 'Rozanne'** although many other gardeners in this book included it too. "It's far and away the best. I put it at the foot of a 'New Dawn' climbing rose and it hides the bare canes," she says. It blooms blue from mid-June to the snow, adds Lorraine, unheard of for a perennial. Plus it doesn't get leggy like so many other geraniums.

"Let the soil feed your plants so you don't have to."

As for walkways, the lazy gardener should use concrete between flagstones to save hours of weeding.

For the sunny garden, Lorraine suggests the following plants:
- Paperbark maple (*Acer griseum*)
- Ninebark shrub *(Physocarpus opulifolius 'Coppertina')*
- Russian sage *(Perovskia atriplicifolia 'Filigran')*
- Summer phlox (*Phlox paniculata 'Shortwood'*)
- Cranesbill geranium (*Geranium 'Rozanne'*)
- Flame grass (*Miscanthus 'Purpurascens'*)
- Species tulips (*Tulipa tarda, turkestanica,* or *clusiana* 'Lady Jane')
- Brazilian verbena *(Verbena bonariensis)*

Paperbark maple is a showstopper. The detail is in its exfoliating bark with shades of cinnamon and texture throughout the year. The **ninebark shrub 'Coppertina'** has coppery foliage and its rosy-pink flower is a bonus. Some ninebarks on the market, such as 'Diablo', are susceptible to mildew, but 'Coppertina' is not.

The **flame grass** needs a lot of space, Lorraine warns, but it adds drama and has fabulous orange-red fall plumes.

Lorraine believes the *Gardening from a Hammock* gardener should invest in tulips that "perennialize." "Most showy tulips fade out, but the wild species tulips, like *Tulipa tarda, turkestanica* and *clusiana* multiply and you get a hit of early spring colour year after year." Her favourite is the **'Lady Jane' tulip.**

The **Brazilian verbena** adds interest and colour when sprinkled throughout the garden and requires no care. Lorraine explains that *Verbena bonariensis* means "good for nothing" verbena, but she likes it because it is tall and acts like a scrim through which you can see.

For the shade garden, Lorraine recommends the following plants:
- 'Golden Shadows' pagoda dogwood (*Cornus alternifolia* 'Golden Shadows')

Verbena bonariensis

Alchemilla mollis

Geranium 'Rozanne'

Cimicifuga simplex 'Hillside Black Beauty'

Kirengeshoma palmata

- Yellow waxbells (*Kirengeshoma palmata*)
- Coral bells (*Heuchera* 'Lime Rickey')
- Siberian bugloss (*Brunnera macrophylla* 'Jack Frost')
- Hosta (*Hosta* 'June')
- Bigroot cranesbill (*Geranium macrorrhizum*)
- Black snakeroot or black bugbane (*Cimicifuga simplex* 'Hillside Black Beauty')
- Lady's mantle (*Alchemilla mollis*)
- Virgin's bower clematis (*Clematis virginiana*)
- White barrenwort or bishop's hat (*Epimedium × youngianum* 'Niveum')

'Golden Shadows' pagoda dogwood likes growing under other trees, providing a valuable function. It has the typical pagoda dogwood horizontal branching pattern and has variegated leaves that have dark green in the centre and chartreuse at the edges. Its distinct veining is a feature.

Yellow waxbells clump nicely within a couple of years, and with their five-foot height, they work well in the mid- or back border. A waxy yellow flower appears in August.

Lorraine's favourite chartreuse colour can be found in **heuchera 'Lime Rickey'**. Lorraine combines it with the yellow waxbells for a golden corner in her backyard.

Nothing performs like **brunnera 'Jack Frost'**, says Lorraine. "I have tried four other varieties of brunnera and 'Jack Frost' is the best. It lights up the area. I like it because it is vigorous. It is great to have the satisfaction that something is responding so well. The colour and shape shimmers in the shade, and the small blue flowers are a bonus in the spring."

The **'June' hosta** has a blue-green leaf with darker edges. Lorraine describes it as "a sea-wave undulating-like combination of greens."

The **geranium macrorrhizum** works for everyone. It can grow in shady, dry areas that are generally hostile to nearly everything else. "You don't have to do anything," expounds Lorraine. "I plant it, it grows and it spreads and asks nothing more of me. It bounces back. I love the pungent scent of its leaves." It has white or pink flowers depending on the variety.

The tall white flowers resembling a bottlebrush spike endear **black snakeroot** to Lorraine, especially since their fragrant blooms last from the late summer through early fall. The lacy foliage adds to their delicate influence.

Lady's mantle is a self-seeder, says Lorraine. The soft green, scalloped leaves form a cup shape that holds tiny drops of water after a rain. This hardy plant produces chartreuse sprays of flowers in June.

Although clematis don't usually do well in the shade, Lorraine has *Clematis virginiana* in her garden. She appreciates its tiny spray of star-like flowers from July through September.

White barrenwort is a favourite of many Master Gardeners. Lorraine loves it because, despite its "delicate elegance, it is tough as nails." It has a fine white flower in spring and does well as a groundcover.

Master Gardener Lorraine Flanigan is editor of Trellis, the magazine of the Toronto Botanical Garden. She also has her own blog, citygardeningonline.com and Tweets @citygardening.

An Aristocratic Garden

Marion Jarvie collects aristocrats. That's what the Master Gardener, worldwide lecturer and teacher calls the plants that thrive in her award-winning garden in Thornhill, Ontario. Those are the only kinds of plants that Marion will recommend.

"I would never dream of having a plant I wouldn't be proud to own," she explains. She rates every plant by several criteria, including interest for more than one season, in more than one area. "A plant should be

"A plant should be beautiful in terms of leaves, bark, flowers and seeds."

beautiful in terms of leaves, bark, flowers and seeds." It gets more points if it attracts birds or butterflies, has fragrance and an artistic shape.

Although the plant selection is regal, the way to achieve the look is simple. "Add three cubic feet of triple mix (a mixture of equal parts of topsoil, peat, compost and sometimes manure). Throw the plants in," Marion says, with the caveat that no matter how hardy these plants are, they need to be well watered their first couple of seasons.

"Watering should be deep – consider watering for 90 minutes, but only once a week," she suggests. As a general guide, she advises gardeners to use an amount of water that's the equivalent to the size of pot the plant came in. For instance, if the plant is in a one-gallon pot, it requires one gallon of water once a week, assuming it has not rained all week. And rain doesn't mean a drizzle, but a soaking downpour.

"It is difficult to overwater and simple to underwater in the summer," she says. "It

Cornus kousa 'Wolf Eyes'

- Water deeply once a week to encourage deep root growth.
- To water, use an amount of water equivalent to the size of the pot the plant came in.
- Fast-growing plants can get out of hand, choose plants that grow slowly to minimize maintenance.
- Don't fight with your shade; embrace it and select shade-tolerant plants with colourful leaves, interesting shapes and texture.

is not our cold winters, but rather under-watering that causes the loss of most plants."

Plant selections are for the sunny garden, but these plants can also handle light shade as long as there are four to five hours of sun.

- Weeping purple beech (*Fagus sylvatica* 'Purple Fountain')
- Blue Colorado spruce (*Picea pungens* 'Montgomery')
- Variegated cornelian cherry dogwood (*Cornus mas* 'Variegata')
- Cranesbill geranium (*Geranium* 'Rozanne')
- Stonecrop (*Sedum* 'Purple Emperor')
- Golden sword yucca (*Yucca filifera* 'Golden Sword')

"Watering should be deep - consider watering for 90 minutes, but only once a week."

Marion describes the **weeping purple beech** as a "truly vertical aristocratic tree that looks exactly as if a jet of water from a fountain is shooting up." Purple leaves make the tree even more dramatic.

In contrast, Marion teams it with a **blue Colorado spruce,** which has an irregular mounded shape and silvery-blue foliage. This is ideal for the lazy gardener as it is slow-growing.

Less common is the early flowering **variegated cornelian cherry dogwood,**

with yellow flowers, followed by red, edible berries in late summer. Its green and white leaves provide the only white in the grouping so Marion emphasizes that it is important to select this variegated variety.

Geranium 'Rozanne' is a favourite because it provides large violet-blue flowers and two-toned green foliage that bloom non-stop from June to October. In its second year, these sprawling plants (buy three) will spread 90 to 175 cm.

Add the hardy **sedum 'Purple Emperor'** with its leaves so deep purple that they look black. The contrast will be dramatic.

The yellow flowers of the **cornelian cherry** work well with the dramatic **golden sword yucca**. This upright plant has golden leaves with a long brilliant green stripe.

"Plant one of each of these plants," says Marion, "and they will stand alone and make a garden you can be proud of."

No matter how much you crave an instant garden, no matter how little time you have to take care of it and no matter how horticulturally challenged you are, you can create a spectacular garden. But don't rush in, Marion warns.

"Grabbing something easy is a big mistake, grabbing something fast growing is also a problem. Choose things that last, grow slowly and don't overdo it."

It's all about texture, shape and foliage, explains Marion, and illustrates that even for the laziest of us, there is no need for compromise with the species and choices available for the shade garden.

Her choices for the shady garden include:
- Red-leafed Japanese maple (*Acer palmatum* 'Emperor 1')

- Compact bronze Hinoki cypress (*Chamaecyparis obtusa* 'Pygmaea Aurescens')
- Kousa dogwood (*Cornus kousa* 'Wolf Eyes' or 'Samaritan')
- Tree peony hybrids (*Paeonia suffruticosa*)
- Hellebore or Lenten rose (*Helleborus × hybridus* 'Royal Heritage')
- Bowles' golden sedge (*Carex elata* 'Aurea')
- Maidenhair fern (*Adiantum pedatum*)

NEW *Helleborus × hybridus* 'Marion Jarvie'

Cornus mas 'Variegata'

Sedum 'Purple Emperor'

Marion illustrates why she uses only what she terms "aristocratic plants" and what others call showpieces.

The **red-leafed Japanese maple** is a small tree that grows in horizontal planes, providing a graceful shape. In fall, it blazes with vibrant colour. In winter, its arching shape becomes a dominant feature. Marion recommends that the lazy gardener underplant it with the mounding form of the **compact bronze Hinoki cypress**. This shrub has flat, fan-shaped foliage, which contrasts well with the lacy foliage of the maple. In spring, the cypress has yellow-bronze leaves, which turn to yellow-green in summer and coppery-bronze in winter. It is especially good for the busy person, explains Marion, because yellow shrubs typically won't grow as vigorously as do green ones and require less maintenance and pruning.

She favours a **kousa dogwood**, either *Cornus kousa* 'Wolf Eyes' or 'Samaritan', which are both variegated and have the same white flowers. The dogwood provides three-season interest and is slow-growing. As a bonus, it bears lovely raspberry-like, edible fruit and the leaves turn scarlet in fall.

The **tree peony** has "drop-dead gorgeous, huge blooms in June," says Marion, "and

it doesn't matter what colour you choose as it only blooms for a short period." The blooms are spectacular. As an added bonus, it also has very attractive foliage, especially in fall when the edges of the leaves turn a bright or rusty red.

The **hellebores** are special for Marion. "They are one of the most important early perennials," she explains. "The **Lenten rose** variety is a super-hardy, cold-loving plant that comes from shaded mountain regions. It grows early and blooms for

"Grabbing something easy is a big mistake, grabbing something fast growing is also a problem. Choose things that last, grow slowly and don't overdo it."

a long time, beginning during Lent when no other perennial is through the ground." She recommends that gardeners start with three plants – make sure they are a named variety – as they have deep-rooted systems and eventually the three original plants will provide as many as 50 blooms, although they may be slow to develop. Hellebores come in white, cream, pink, rose, red and maroon, often with contrasting spots. She recommends grouping plants that flower in shades of rose and pink. They will form a tough clump of leathery evergreen leaves.

Marion describes her next choice, **Bowles' golden sedge**, as a "lovely shade grass, that comes out like a sparkler." It provides brilliant, lemony foliage all season. Her final choice, the native **maidenhair fern**, will mislead you. It looks dainty because of its delicate foliage, but it is tough, tolerates drought and adds bright green foliage as well as texture to the garden.

Marion Jarvie consults, lectures and showcases her award-winning garden at 37 Thornheights Road, Thornhill, Ontario L3T 3L9 four weekends a year. Explore more at www.marionjarvie.ca.

A Drought Tolerant Garden

The mother-son team of Jeff and Marjorie Mason have grown Mason House Gardens in Uxbridge, Ontario, into one of the most well-respected nurseries in the province. Not bad considering that even though Jeff loves collecting plants, he hates gardening.

As Marjorie retreats a little from working in the nursery to focus more on running garden tours, lecturing and perhaps updating her 1999 book, *Amazing Annuals*, Jeff continues producing thousands of perennials, favouring interesting and unusual species.

Marjorie worked for 20 years in a Pickering, Ontario, nursery, ultimately running the greenhouse, where more than 550 kinds of geraniums were grown. Jeff started working at the nursery, packing and loading bags of soil when he was 13, eventually working with his mother as assistant manager. "If something unusual came in, we had to have it," he recalls.

While working at the nursery, Marjorie bought a house and property in nearby Uxbridge. She bought the house in the winter, and couldn't know that the soil was all sand and that the well could not provide irrigation.

Necessity being the mother of invention, she and Jeff found a solution that has worked for them ever since and which only now is becoming popular: **xeriscape gardening, gardening that requires no watering regardless of how hot and sunny it is.**

Xeriscaping turned out to be a blessing for Jeff because it minimizes the amount of work necessary in the garden.

"I hate gardening. I collect plants. I install them but I don't tinker in the garden. I hate weeding. I took out all the grass in my lawn at home and I only touch the plants when absolutely necessary. After

- Russian stonecrop (*Sedum kamtschaticum* 'Weihenstephaner Gold')
- Bloody cranesbill (*Geranium sanguineum* var. *striatum*)
- Blue sea holly (*Eryngium planum*)
- Eastern blue star (*Amsonia tabernaemontana*)
- Trailing verbenas

working in the nursery all day, I have no interest in gardening." He plans his garden accordingly. For example, he doesn't dead-head his spring bulbs but instead plants perennials nearby to emerge in time to hide the bulbs and their dying foliage.

Both mother and son love unusual and new plants. Their nursery now features more than 1,000 varieties. They offer eight varieties of elephant ears and 40 different colours of coleus. For *Gardening from a Hammock*, however, they wanted to demonstrate how to plant for a low-maintenance xeriscape garden. In their hot, sunny garden, they grow plants that need no water. Ever.

Although their garden is in sand, they also have produced xeriscape gardens in clay soil using the same plants.

For the sunny garden, the Masons recommend these plants:
- Swiss stone pine (*Pinus cembra*)
- Compact Andorra juniper (*Juniperus horizontalis* 'Plumosa Compacta')
- Mugo pine (*Pinus mugo* var. *pumilio*)
- Pasque flower (*Pulsatilla vulgaris*)
- Little bluestem grass (*Schizachyrium scoparium* 'The Blues')
- English lavender (*Lavandula angustifolia* 'Munstead')
- Prairie dropseed (*Sporobolus heterolepis*)

The **Swiss stone pine** stops you in your tracks when you walk by it in the Mason garden. It is the narrowest of the upright pines in a columnar shape. This slow-growing specimen sports yellow tips in winter and is drought resistant.

> *"I hate weeding. I took out all the grass in my lawn at home and I only touch the plants when absolutely necessary."*

Another evergreen that creates winter interest is the **compact Andorra juniper**. "It is one of the best groundcovers for hill-sides," explains Jeff. Once it is established the evergreen grows densely, softening the rain hitting the ground and helping to avoiding erosion. It has a very soft texture of blue-green foliage that turns plum-purple in the fall and winter.

The Masons select the **mugo pine** because it is easy and durable and requires only a light trim every few years. The compact bush, with its dwarf globular shape, is evergreen year-round.

Pasque flower is the first plant to bloom at the end of March, and Marjorie would love it for that reason alone. As a bonus, it has beautiful fuzzy seed heads, which she describes as puffs of smoke. It self-seeds and is great untended in the garden. "It carpets the entire area in blue-violet, purple flowers. From one plant I now have hundreds. They have created their own drifts," Marjorie explains.

Lavandula angustifolia 'Munstead'

Jeff considers the **little bluestem grass** "one of the best medium-sized grasses for dry, sandy areas." He explains that it likes being dry and flops in wet soil. It has upright clumps of steely blue foliage with silvery seed heads. When it gets cool, the entire plant turns purple and orange. "It's stunning," he says.

"In spring **lavender** looks like a scrungy mess of dead leaves, but we wait until the weather warms, see where the new shoots are coming and cut it back there, but never to the ground," advises Jeff. "Lavender has all the basics," Marjorie adds, "silver foliage, beautiful blue flowers, fragrance, and is one of the most drought-resistant plants."

Eryngium planum

Prairie dropseed is a native grass that forms clumps of fine-textured, hair-like foliage with arching leaves, says Marjorie, adding, "you want to touch it." In fall, the green leaves turn gold and pumpkin colours. "When you walk through it in mass plantings, it smells like buttered popcorn," says Jeff.

Aster divaricatus

"It could even be a lawn substitute," interjects Marjorie.

Underplanting **Prairie dropseed** with **Russian stonecrop** creates a lovely contrast, says Jeff, as the sedum produces a carpet of dark green plants with coppery stems and in June they are covered with masses of golden-yellow flowers. If the area is dry, it is non-invasive and "always looks good," he adds.

Bloody cranesbill is a dwarf perennial geranium with soft pink flowers that have red veins in spring. More colour is provided in the fall, when the leaves turn a reddish colour. It grows in dark green mounds and is used as filler for parts of the garden where colour is needed.

Hosta 'Blue Angel'

The bright blue, thistle-like flower of the **blue sea holly** is unlike any other flower shape, according to Marjorie. "This plant adds structure you don't get from any other flowers. It's also interesting after flowering because the thistles remain."

Eastern blue star is actually a star for three seasons. Icy-blue flower clusters bloom in late spring to early summer. Jeff explains that once the flower heads have bloomed, clusters of new shoots emerge, hiding the spent blooms; later, the narrow, glossy willow-like foliage turns gold in autumn.

Marjorie considers annuals the crowning jewels in the garden and has to include at least one, **trailing verbena.** These plants are commonly seen in containers, where they need daily watering, but in the garden, once established, she says that they never need watering. She suggests any kind as they come in a large assort-

"Lavender has all the basics — silver foliage, beautiful blue flowers, fragrance, and is one of the most drought-resistant plants."

ment of colours but recommends looking at the Proven Winners website for specific varieties.

"We rarely use them in containers because they are so superior in the ground," she says. Just a small pot will give nearly a square metre of colour and they are easy to look after.

Dry shade is one of the most difficult areas in which to garden, but Marjorie and Jeff look to their own xeriscape garden for answers. Their plant picks for the dry, shady garden include these:
- Hosta (*Hosta* 'Blue Angel')
- Barrenwort or bishop's hat (*Epimedium × perralchicum* 'Frohnleiten')
- Spirea (*Spirea × bumalda* 'Goldflame')

Chasmanthium latifolium

- Northern sea oats (*Chasmanthium latifolium*)
- Bigroot cranesbill (*Geranium macrorrhizum* 'Ingwersen's Variety')
- Creeping Japanese sedge (*Carex morrowii* 'Ice Dance')
- White wood aster (*Aster divaricatus*)
- Black snakeroot or black bugbane (*Cimicifuga simplex* 'Hillside Black Beauty')

"We have to start with **hostas**," says Jeff, "and '**Blue Angel**' or any other hosta with thick waxy leaves holds up to drought. The waxy coating doesn't allow moisture out of the leaves. It also makes the plant more slug-resistant."

He also favours any **barrenwort** as an evergreen groundcover but has selected the '**Frohnleiten**' variety for its buttery-yellow flowers in spring. "They look graceful with wonderful sprays of flowers in early spring, but they are tough," confirms Marjorie. The foliage looks good all season, and they are "more or less" evergreen.

> *"Any hosta with thick waxy leaves holds up to drought. The waxy coating doesn't allow moisture out of the leaves. It also makes the plant more slug-resistant."*

The dwarf '**Goldflame**' **spirea** shrub does well in semi-shade and is drought resistant. When it emerges, the foliage is a burnt orange, says Jeff, and then it turns green when the plant has pink-red flowers in July. In the fall it returns to its flame colour.

One of few grasses that thrive in the shade, **northern sea oats** also provides lots of interest. Marjorie says that the grass clumps are reminiscent of bamboo, while Jeff likens the drooping showy flower head clusters to dangling goldfish crackers. (Warning: the grass will reseed with abandon in moist soil but has not been invasive in their dry garden where it has thrived for the past 15 years. They only cut it back in the spring because it provides winter interest.)

The Masons like their choice of **bigroot cranesbill** because it will grow in the driest, shadiest and crummiest areas. It is a vigorous but not invasive spreader and is weed proof, but it will make room for large plants like hostas. "It is the workhorse of our dry shady garden," says Marjorie. Its pink flowers start blooming in late spring and the leaves are very fragrant.

The **creeping Japanese sedge 'Ice Dance'** is as "fresh and green in January as it is in August," says Jeff. "It looks like someone took a bunch of spider plants and plunked them in the ground." This spurge spreads but is not invasive. It has white creamy variegation with a relatively fine texture.

Another tough groundcover for dry shady areas is the **white wood aster**. It produces tiny masses of starry white flowers with yellow centres from August through September.

Black snakeroot or **black bugbane** blooms in the late summer or early fall with 150-cm spikes topped with a fragrant white blush. "It perfumes the whole garden," says Marjorie. She has five clumps of it in her garden.

Mother and son team, Marjorie and Jeff Mason, run Mason House Gardens in Uxbridge, Ontario, a nursery with more than 1500 plant varieties. They also lecture and Marjorie can be heard Saturday mornings hosting her garden radio show on CKDO, Oshawa, Ontario. Check out their ornamental and heirloom veggies at www.masonhousegardens.com.

Gardening from a Hammock
with Martin Galloway

A Naturalist's Garden

Martin Galloway does not water his plants, which may surprise many gardeners. What makes this policy even more controversial is that he has thousands of plants on his 17-acre Chalk Lake Greenhouses in Uxbridge, Ontario. He grows acres and acres of field stock, specializing in perennials, including native flowers, and does not water except during the initial planting. Even then he likes to plant before or during a rain. Although Martin runs this popular nursery, he is first and foremost a botanist and a naturalist.

"I am really interested in all plants, because of all the other life forms they attract."

"I am really interested in all plants, because of all the other life forms they attract. I have no lineup of good and bad guys. I like to see all the weird things happening, the unusual ways to meet and

greet, how they defend themselves, the on-going competition among creatures. I like to see them in action.

"I interpret something through basic principles of biology – where the plant comes from, and what its role is in nature. Then I can see where it will work."

Martin teaches this and much more as a patho-physiology, evolutionary biology and genetics teacher at Seneca College and formerly at York University. He also has hosted two television programs, *The Secret World of Gardens* and *Harrowsmith Country Life*. "I love teaching and I love horticulture," Martin declares. "It's my life, not my work."

His nursery doesn't have a watering system at all. The decision about whether to use water "depends what you are trying to achieve," he explains. Plants grown without additional water develop differ-

Sedum rupestre 'Angelina'

Sedum sieboldii

ent tissues. Their leaves are smaller, and bushier and there is a waxy cuticle on the surface. When they grow in drier conditions, they adapt to those conditions. The plants won't be as big and lush as plants that are watered regularly but they also won't need as much nutrition and will be less prone to fungal and bacterial infections and insect infestations. "If I lose a plant," he says, "it's because I put it in the wrong place."

For a low-maintenance, no-watering, no-weeding, no-mowing yet different and interesting sunny garden, Martin suggests a full sedum lawn. He recommends planting 20 different species in wide patches or colonies, creating designs such as dry stream beds or meandering swaths in a flowing pattern. He explains that it is easy to propagate these plants: pick them up and put them directly into soil. "You never need to water. Weed initially until they form a mat and then weeds won't grow through."

He suggests adding some other plants, such as geraniums, bellflowers, tiny strawberry plants and evening primrose for interest. He proposes taller sedums to poke through the low-growing ones in late summer. As well, he suggests saxifrage, sempervivums and alpine plants that will complement the sedum garden.

"The sedum lawn will have few pests and will be a nectar source for all butterflies, bees and shimmering flies. It is much more interesting than grass," says Martin.

Plants for the sunny sedum lawn include:
- Stonecrop (*Sedum rupestre* 'Angelina')
- Autumn stonecrop (*Sedum telephium* 'Matrona')
- White-flowered bellflower (*Campanula rotundifolia* 'White Gem')
- Blue bells of Scotland (*Campanula rotundifolia*)
- Stonecrop (*Sedum reflexum* 'Blue Spruce')
- Dwarf cransebill (*Geranium × cantabrigiense* 'Cambridge')
- October Daphne or stonecrop (*Sedum sieboldii*)
- Evening primrose or Ozark sundrop (*Oenothera missouriensis*)
- Ornamental strawberry (*Fragaria vesca* 'Lipstick')
- Russian stonecrop (*Sedum kamtschaticum*)
- Stonecrop hybrids (*Sedum* 'Autumn Joy', 'Brilliant', 'Jaws', 'Postman's Pride', 'Rosy Glow', 'Vera Jameson')
- Baby tears stonecrop or Swedish stonecrop (*Sedum album* 'Faro Form')
- Two-row stonecrop (*Sedum spurium* 'Dragon's Blood, 'John Creech', 'Red Carpet' or 'Voodoo')

The stonecrops Martin selects create variations in texture, foliage and colour and are tough enough to walk on. The mounding or rosette shapes present minimum surface area for water loss. Some varieties

"Sedums work well in any combination or on their own."

grow into a carpet, others are upright ornamental specimens, but all have thick, fleshy, succulent leaves and divide well. Seed heads of the taller varieties provide winter interest and food for birds.

Stonecrop 'Angelina' is a low evergreen groundcover that forms a trailing mat of golden-yellow leaves. Clusters of yellow starry flowers appear during the hot summer.

A favourite, **'Matrona' autumn stonecrop**, was Perennial Plant of the Year 2000 in Holland for its robust and well-rounded form. In the spring, the flowers start out as light green, colouring to rosy-pink, and by fall turn a bronze colour. The leaves are grey-green with rosy edges on dark burgundy stems.

The **white-flowered bellflowers** prefer wetter spots. Their delicate white and bright blue flowers offer colour in the sedum garden and bloom throughout the summer. Martin enjoys their round leaves. For colour in sun or shade, Martin recommends **blue bells of Scotland**, bright blue, bell-shaped flowers that blossom from June through September.

'Blue Spruce' stonecrop has yellow flowers midsummer with a grey-green leaf. Its almost spruce-like leaves are arranged in whorls of six leaves. The evergreen **dwarf 'Cambridge' cranesbill** is a perfect filler and contrast to the sedums with its pink blooms, which appear in late spring through to early summer. The leaves are attractively lobed and have a distinctive aroma.

Sedum telephium 'Matrona'

From August through the fall, **October Daphne** provides pink-purple blooms with contrasting rounded grey-green leaves. The bright flowers of the **evening primrose** glow from late spring to early summer. This quick-spreading plant attracts butterflies. **Ornamental strawberry** brings cherry-red flowers throughout the garden from spring to autumn.

Russian stonecrop forms a carpet of small, scalloped leaves spreading to form a thick patch. It has glossy, deep green leaves and, in early summer, half-inch golden-yellow flowers that open from pink buds. The flowers are star-like and long lasting.

The family of stonecrop hybrids are linked by genus, but each has its own personality. **'Autumn Joy' stonecrop** is one of the more popular sedums, very hardy and drought resistant yet providing interest year-round. This sedum grows in a 30- to 40-cm mound with pink flowers emerging in the late summer, aging to a coppery pink and then to a rust colour in the fall.

In late summer and fall, **'Brilliant' stonecrop** produces large flat clusters of small pink flowers on top of 45-cm tall stems, with blue-green succulent foliage. **'Jaws' stonecrop** forms a blue-green bushy mound. It has heavily serrated leaves that look like shark's teeth. Large heads of dusty salmon-rose flowers appear in late summer, developing into brown seed heads and adding interest to the winter garden.

For blue-purple foliage with a semi-upright habit, Martin selects **'Postman's Pride' stonecrop**, discovered in a Belgian postman's garden. In late summer, deep purple buds open to pink-red flowers that turn burgundy in the fall. **'Rosy Glow' stonecrop** features blue-green, low, mounding foliage and rich ruby-red flowers. **'Vera Jameson' stonecrop** forms a 15- to 20-cm-high, non-spreading clump of powdery, mahogany-purple leaves. In the late summer, pink starry flowers appear, clustered at the ends of each stem.

Baby tears stonecrop or **Swedish stonecrop** has tiny light green leaves that resemble elongated beads sprawled on the ground. The leaves turn shades of red to bronze during the summer and again in winter. Delicate, white, star-shaped flowers appear in summer.

All four varieties of the **two-row stonecrop** are fast-growing groundcovers with various shades of red, red-purple or red-pink flowers and leaves. They work well in any combination or on their own.

Sanguinaria canadensis

Despite his interesting sedum garden choices for low-maintenance sun plants, it is the shade that intrigues Martin. "For low maintenance, pick slow-growing plants," he advises. "Try things and go with what works."

Most trees, shrubs, perennials and groundcovers work for him, and he selects some of the hardiest. Martin's choices for a shady garden include the following:

- Thornless honeylocust tree (*Gleditsia triacanthos inermis*)
- Kentucky coffeetree (*Gymnocladus dioica*)
- Canadian hemlock (*Tsuga canadensis*)
- Japanese kerria (*Kerria japonica*)
- Koreanspice viburnum (*Viburnum carlesii*)
- Variegated zigzag goldenrod (*Solidago flexicaulis* 'Variegata')
- Bloodroot (*Sanguinaria canadensis*)
- Creeping woodland phlox (*Phlox stolonifera* 'Sherwood Purple')
- Mountain lover (*Paxistima canbyi*)
- Canadian wild ginger (*Asarum canadense*)
- Yellow, red and white barrenwort (*Epimedium × versicolor* 'Sulphureum', *Epimedium × rubrum*, *Epimedium × youngianum* 'Niveum')
- Maidenhair fern (*Adiantum pedatum*)
- Christmas fern (*Polystichum acrostichoides*)
- Braun's holly fern (*Polystichum braunii*)
- Ghost fern (*Athyrium* 'Ghost')

Locust trees are preferred because they don't grow very big and are not invasive. Martin identifies the **thornless honeylocust** tree in particular. This is a popular landscaping tree because it is fast growing, has fragrant yellow spring flowers and an open silhouette that lets grass grow underneath. The fruits of the tree are flat brown pods resembling twisted leather straps that can reach 20 cm long. Its small leaves turn yellow and drop, but are easy to use as mulch by simply raking them into the soil.

The **Kentucky coffeetree** is a "cool" tree, according to Martin. He warns against being disappointed at first because it starts off looking like a naked stick. Then the enormous (up to one metre and 60 cm wide) doubly compound leaves appear in late spring. It branches into an open airy form, developing into an odd-branched clubbed structure in the fall. At that time it reveals deeply furrowed bark and, on female trees, 20-cm long, dark brown leathery pods. It is listed as a threatened species under Ontario's Endangered Species Act 2007.

The native **Canadian hemlock** is shade tolerant, slow growing and long lived. One recorded specimen is at least 554 years old. This evergreen has a pyramidal shape with a soft, textured, glossy dark green leaf.

The **Japanese kerria** is very shade tolerant and useful for the four-season interest it gives. It produces bright yellow flowers in late spring, the green foliage turns yellow in autumn and its bright green arching twigs provide winter interest. It blooms off and on all summer (if given enough rain) and is one of the few shrubs that flower in the shade.

The deciduous shrub, **Korean spice viburnum,** works well as a landscaping plant since it grows to only 150 cm and is low maintenance. In spring it is covered with white flowers but its spicy fragrance is what makes it irresistible. Its green foliage turns bright scarlet in mid-autumn.

Native **goldenrod** is a favourite of Martin's because it flowers from late summer to fall when it is harder to find blooms in the garden. The zigzag variety is better behaved than the roadside version as it has fewer tendencies to spread. This plant has wide, yellow-splashed leaves, and the typical yellow flowers emerge above each leaf on the upper part of the stem.

Athyrium 'Ghost'

Adiantum pedatum

Sometimes the stem zigzags from leaf to leaf, thus the name.

As an aside, Martin explains that unlike what many people believe, goldenrod does not cause allergies because it is only insect pollinated. Ragweed, however, flowers at the same time and is the real culprit as it is wind pollinated and causes allergic reactions.

Bloodroot is another favourite native plant, with white flowers early in spring. Its foliage is shaped like a little parasol, says Martin. It dies down in midsummer and is dormant. There is a single leaf for each flower and it curls around the emerging flower, unfurling as the flower blooms. Ants spread the seeds around. The roots contain a blood-red juice, which accounts for the name.

For colour, Martin suggests **phlox**. The '**Sherwood Purple**' cultivar he likes is a good woodland plant that creates a mat of evergreen foliage with a brilliant show of clear purple flowers in spring. However, any phlox will provide a rich carpet of colour.

Martin recommends a large number of groundcovers. **Mountain lover** is one with a red flower in early spring. **Wild ginger**, with its round glossy leaves, is very slow growing. It forms a solid patch of heart-shaped leaves concealing the burgundy flowers that bloom in late spring.

Martin selects three **barrenwort** plants that he considers grossly underused. Each blooms in a different colour. He likes the foliage that has purple hues in the fall and all winter. The old foliage crumples and covers the ground in winter through spring, at which time the new leaves rise above the old in company with the flowers. "It is slow growing but consistent, will live forever, and is drought tolerant and tough," he says. 'Sulphureum' is yellow, the rubrum red and the 'Niveum' white.

Each of the plants is hardy, blooms in the shade and provides excellent groundcover and edging.

Maidenhair ferns are some of the toughest plants Martin knows. "I saw them on Newfoundland Table Mountain where the mountain is toxic to almost every other plant. They survive when it is very hot, extremely cold, and where there are no nutrients in the soil because of metals. They also grow in deep shade beneath giant trees. Although the ferns look delicate and lacy, they are indestructible." The plant has a thin, polished black-coloured main leaf stalk that contrasts with its fan-like sculpted leaflets. An interesting non-relevant fact is that these plants have water-repelling compounds on their foliage so water runs off the leaves, and even when the plant is immersed in water, the leaves remain dry.

Martin also favours **Christmas fern** for its longer evergreen leaves. These asymmetrical ferns have a fine texture and sprout new fiddleheads in the springtime. In addition, he selects **Braun's holly fern** for its tidier foliage. It has dark green shiny fronds with brown ruffles on each edge and an upright arching habit. The fronds arise from a single point, giving the fern a more formal appearance.

Ghost fern is a hybrid between lady fern and Japanese painted fern. Its silver and purple variegation is larger and more robust than the popular painted fern. The plants form upright arching clumps of triangular leaves. The overall appearance of the fern is a light silvery grey-green that inspired the name ghost fern.

Teacher, lecturer and botanist Martin Galloway has a nursery in Uxbridge, Ontario. To read about him, his talks and his plants, google 'Chalk Lake Greenhouses', which specializes in perennials, native and herbaceous plants.

The Uncluttered and Elegant Garden

Mary Fisher's urban backyard reflects clarity of vision, restraint and discipline, illustrating her expertise as a Master Gardener. Although simple in design, her garden gets its richness and interest from texture and the repetition of a small number of select plants.

"It's simple and uncluttered," she says about her garden, "and I am coming around to that in my whole life."

"My garden is simple and uncluttered; and I am coming around to that in my whole life."

A self-proclaimed lifelong learner, Mary worked as a librarian at Queen's Park, Toronto, and didn't garden at all when her three children were young. When they moved to a house with a front garden, she began what became a passion.

"I heard about Master Gardeners and went to the Civic Centre (now Toronto Botanical Garden) to write a test to see if I was even eligible to take the course. I didn't know one answer and handed back the paper. I remembered the questions, studied and wrote the test the following year."

When her family moved into their current home, she ripped out the nondescript bushes and grass, brought in good topsoil and built a retaining wall to create two levels in the sloping backyard. She had recently read a book by gardeners Nori and Sandra Pope called *Colour by Design* that got her interested in creating three squares: red, blue and yellow. "It didn't work at all so I turned it into a regular perennial garden." That still wasn't right for her, so when she and her husband bought a farm, Mary moved all their perennials to the country. She then recreated her city garden in a totally different style.

Euonymus fortunei 'Sarcoxie'

Malus 'Makamik'

"We had redone our house and we wanted our garden to match the modern feel and be less blowsy."

This time, she created four rectangular beds on two levels around a pea-gravel centre. Each quadrant has a featured plant and at least one border within another border. Each small garden can stand alone but they all complement one another.

Her sun plants and combinations include the following:

- Callery pear tree (*Pyrus calleryana* 'Chanticleer')
- Euonymus (*Euonymus fortunei* 'Sarcoxie')
- Fothergilla (*Fothergilla major* 'Mount Airy')
- Flowering Crabapple tree (*Malus* 'Makamik')
- Scotch moss (*Sagina subulata* 'Aurea')
- Pink thrift (*Armeria maritima* 'Dusseldorf Pride')

Mary initially planted three **callery pear trees** at the back of her property to create a screen with these tall, thin beauties. "Pear trees are so hardy that they prosper throughout the city of New York," explains Mary. "They have great spring white blossoms that look like clouds. They are ornamental with beautiful shiny green leaves, and yellow colour in the fall. Since they are columnar, they are ideal for a small space."

At the bottom of the garden is a hedge of **euonymus** that grows to about 50 cm. Dark green in colour, this tough plant withstands considerable shade and challenging city conditions. Behind that, Mary has planted five or six **fothergillas** that act as a taller border. The shrub fothergilla provides lush white, bottlebrush-shaped flowers in early spring, but what Mary really loves about these bushes is their "sea of flames" in the fall.

Gracing one wall is an **espalier crabapple tree** providing an abundance of pink showy flowers in the spring and tiny crabapples in the fall, which the birds immediately devour.

In the middle garden are two rectangular beds. Again Mary repeats the border-within-a-border pattern. In one bed is a border of **scotch moss** with its acid-green colour, surrounding a centre of **pink thrift**. The moss has small white flowers in May through June and a dense rounded tuft shape that forms soft mossy carpets. The pink thrift showcases hundreds of pink blooms from June through July and then forms compact evergreen mounds. Mary especially likes the pink against the bright acid green.

Although Mary could add more plant suggestions for the sunny garden, the ones she chose are the ones she uses. By adding

"I love the fothergilla because it's a sea of flames in the fall."

others to her own garden, she would risk losing the uncluttered, clean and symmetrical look. She has learned by trial and error, and although she freely admits that a garden is never done, she also doesn't want to "over-do" it anymore.

Mary's plant suggestions for a shady garden include these:

- Baltic ivy (*Hedera helix* 'Baltica')
- Kousa dogwood (*Cornus kousa* 'Satomi')
- Boxwood (*Buxus microphylla* 'Green Mountain')
- Lady's mantle (*Alchemilla mollis*)
- Japanese blood grass (*Imperata cylindrica* 'Red Baron')

Fothergilla major 'Mount Airy'
(fall colours)

The yard requires little work and yet provides year-round interest and contrast with its relatively few plants and its geometric patterns. The **Baltic ivy** is arranged in a rectangular bed with three **dogwoods** in the centre. A path has been constructed with pea gravel and is bordered by **boxwood**.

The three dogwood trees provide large pink springtime blossoms over green foliage that turns crimson in fall. What makes these small trees exceptional is their horizontal branches. The boxwood and Baltic ivy provide different heights of green on green, border on border continu-

ing the geometric shape. The effect is striking and elegant.

Another dramatic quadrant features chartreuse **lady's mantle** outlining a square with contrasting red **Japanese blood grass** inside. The lady's mantle with its scalloped leaf shape and soft green colour is the rectangular border behind which the dramatic red of the Japanese blood grass emerges. "I chose the grass for its red colour in the fall," Mary explains.

"When the sun shines on it, it is breathtaking," she says. "Look for these moments in your garden. You have to slow down to do it – it's hard, but worth it."

Master Gardener Mary Fisher is the 2010-2012 co-chair of the Board of Directors, Toronto Botanical Garden. She is a former coordinator of Toronto Master Gardeners and remains an enthusiastic city and country gardener.

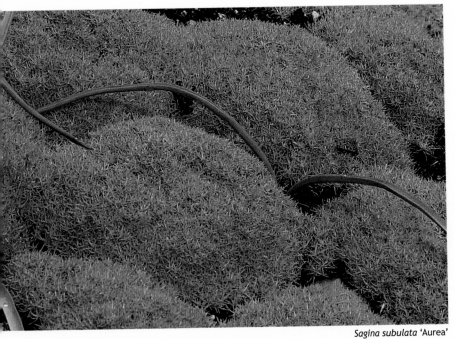

Sagina subulata 'Aurea'

The Plantaholic's Garden

When Master Gardener Merle Burston moved into her home, she knew exactly how to create a new garden. She buried the existing clay subsoil with 100 yards of top-grade soil, creating 60-cm-deep raised beds. "Good soil is the backbone of the garden," she says.

As an active member and past co-ordinator of Toronto Master Gardeners and former chair of the Ontario Rock Garden

"Good soil is the backbone of the garden."

Society, it is not surprising that Merle had no problem filling her new garden beds.

"I had the best time selecting and choosing plants with lots of help from friends," she says. Yet when asked to select a combination of plants for the garden-

ing challenged, she had difficulty. The problem wasn't which ones to choose, it was which to leave out. "I love them all," she sighs. "To me, a garden is about life. I stop in my tracks to look at the new red leaves of the maple. It's magic listening to the birds chattering in the trees. I get so excited when I see the tips of new spring growth poking through the earth."

How to choose? The solution is to select the must-haves, the ones that Merle cannot imagine living without.

In the sunny garden, these include the following:
- Butterfly bush (*Buddleia davidii* 'Potter's Purple')
- Bluebeard (*Caryopteris × clandonensis* 'Kew Blue')
- Maiden grass (*Miscanthus sinensis* 'Morning Light')

61

TIPS

❧ *Plant tall grasses like miscanthus in front of bulbs to hide spent leaves.*

❧ *Good soil is the backbone of the garden.*

- Wild peony or Balkan peony (*Paeonia mascula*) or any species peony
- Oriental poppy (*Papaver orientale*)
- Flanders poppy (*Papaver rhoeas*)
- Red Bor kale (*Brassica oleracea* 'Red Bor')
- Mexican sunflower (*Tithonia rotundifolia* 'Torch')

Merle chose the **'Potter's Purple' butterfly bush** not only for its appealing flower, but also for the fact that it attracts the Monarch butterfly to the garden, as it provides food for the butterfly on its migration. Another advantage to this shrub is that its dark purple flowers bloom from mid-July until frost.

She favours the bushy upright **'Kew Blue' bluebeard shrub** because it provides dark blue flowers in late summer and fall, its silvery leaves are scented and it also attracts butterflies.

"I love grasses," says Merle, who has trouble singling out only one favourite. She selects **maiden grass** because of its arching shape, variegation and the way light spills through the leaves. "It's in motion and vibrant," she explains. "As well, after it flowers at the end of the season, the grass turns a straw colour and provides interest all winter. And it doesn't self-seed." She suggests planting grasses in front of bulbs, because the grasses will emerge when the bulbs' flowers are spent, hiding the leaves.

Brassica oleracea 'Red Bor'

The **wild peony** also has a lot going for it, but make sure you select the species variety, Merle cautions. It has a single flower so it is not top heavy and doesn't flop like the more common varieties. Its cut leaves provide a good background for other plants later in the season. Like most perennials, its glorious flower lasts only a couple of weeks, but the seed head then ripens and splits into an interesting form that lasts until September. Although lazy gardeners need not bother, Merle collects the seeds ("They look like iridescent black pearls.") to plant or donate to a seed exchange.

"I love the texture and form of the Japanese painted fern. With something like this growing in the shade, who needs flowers?"

Throughout her home, Merle has photos and illustrations of **poppies** and admits that she likes everything about them, "their shape, brilliance of colour, and the papery petals." She appreciates how their leaves disappear after the plant flowers in late spring and summer. Merle also lets annual poppies self-seed, filling in during the summer with orange and red throughout the garden. "It's so easy, you don't have to do anything," she adds.

"In late September, many of us stick those ubiquitous purple cabbages in our gardens, but Merle suggests looking for a variety that's a bit different. The **Red Bor kale** is a tall variety that is tall (about 1 m) and deeply frilled with curly leaves. She loves its texture, its contrast and its animated purple colour.

"If it's new, different, then that's what I want to add to my garden," Merle says.

Chelone lyonii 'Hot Lips'

Hydrangea paniculata 'Limelight'

Athyrium niponicum 'Pictum'

She discovered the annual **Mexican sunflower** about 15 years ago. "It was something unusual in a catalogue. I've been growing it ever since. They start out as puny little things and it seems like they reach six feet almost overnight, and then flower until frost." The Mexican sunflower grows very tall (1.5 m) and asserts itself with bright red-orange flowers from behind grasses and other plants. It has a soft fuzzy leaf and can be grown easily from seed.

"I'll try anything I haven't grown before," says Merle, "but there are some plants that I simply have to have." For the shady garden, Merle Burston, as with any loving guardian, finds it hard to choose one plant over another when drawing up a list of recommendations.

She again opted for the plants that are basic necessities in the garden, her "must-haves," the garden workhorses, and plants that provide continuous beauty and pleasure.

Her selections for the shady garden include these:

- Golden Japanese forest grass (*Hakonechloa macra* 'Aureola')
- Pink turtlehead (*Chelone lyonii* 'Hot Lips')
- Toad lily (*Tricyrtis hirta* 'Miyazaki')
- Japanese painted fern (*Athyrium niponicum* 'Pictum')
- Hydrangea (*Hydrangea paniculata* 'Limelight')
- Lady's mantle (*Alchemilla mollis*)
- Hydrangea (*Hydrangea arborescens* 'Annabelle')
- Azure monkshood (*Aconitum carmichaelii* 'Wilsonii')

The **golden Japanese forest grass** has arching foliage that cascades like a waterfall. Its long leaf blades are striped with bright yellow and slender green lines and work magically with a golden hosta nearby to make the colour jump out. "It's nice to grow this near hostas because they contrast in texture and shape," Merle says. "The grass is fine whereas most hostas have substance to them."

The native **pink turtlehead** is fun: you can pinch them open like a snapdragon. This plant provides pink flowers late in the summer and shiny dark green leaves all season. It also is a hummingbird magnet and is deer resistant.

The starry burgundy-spotted white flowers of the **toad lily** bloom down its stem in autumn. It is another vibrant late-season plant.

The **Japanese painted fern** is a favourite because each one is slightly different. "However many I have, each one has a different colour and pattern," says Merle. "I love the texture and form. With something like this growing in the shade, who needs flowers?"

The **'Limelight' hydrangea** provides – you guessed it – lime-coloured accent in the garden, which bounces back to other plants, especially the lady's mantle. Large globular heads flower from midsummer until frost and provide winter interest. Please note: this shrub prefers some sun to properly show off. Merle advises to try **'Annabelle' hydrangea** for deep shade. It has round snowball-shaped flowers in creamy white, which turn green as they ripen late in the season, then become straw-coloured over the winter.

Even though all parts of **monkshood** are poisonous, Merle loves it because it is reliable, doesn't flop, is tall (1.5 m)

Hakonechloa macra 'Aureola'

and produces deep purple-blue spikes in early autumn. She has five plantings of it. Its name refers to its hooded or helmet-shaped flowers.

Merle has divided and moved clumps of **lady's mantle** liberally throughout her garden. "I love the beads of water on the leaves after a rain," she says. Its lime-green spray of flowers at the end of June accents the mound-shaped scalloped green leaves.

The essentials in a shade garden only begin with this list, insists Merle. "Of course, you have to have dogwoods, hostas, ferns, hellebores, primulas, trilliums, and there are so many more…"

But for us lazy gardeners, that's enough.

Papaver orientale

Master Gardener Merle Burston was coordinator of the Toronto Master Gardeners. She is former chair and an enthusiastic member of the Ontario Rock Garden & Hardy Plant Society plus an active volunteer at the Toronto Botanical Garden.

A Relaxing Garden

As director of horticulture for the Toronto Botanical Garden, Paul Zammit never stops thinking about plants, lecturing about plants, working with plants. However, this isn't something new for this energetic dynamo, since that's exactly what he did for 20 years as perennial plant manager at Plant World Ltd. in Toronto.

"When you grow up, you've got to love your job," he says, laughing. "When I get home after a full day at work, I go work in my garden. It relaxes me."

Know how much time you are willing to commit to your garden. Be realistic about your physical abilities."

As Paul considers and discards dozens of plants perfect for *Gardening from a Hammock,* he pleads to add other, less hardy specimens and more of his favourites. "There is no such thing as a maintenance-free garden," he insists. Yet he has no difficulty selecting plants that can withstand some neglect, little pruning or deadheading, and drought while creating interesting and unusual features year-round.

He encourages gardeners to be observant and honest, first about their garden conditions, then about themselves. "Know not only where and when the sun hits, what type of soil you have, but also how much time you are willing to commit to your garden. Be realistic about your physical abilities.

"Start small. Don't become overwhelmed. Take a class, read some books. In this digital age, go around your neighbourhood and take pictures of plants you like. Go to a public garden. Start small and add year after year," he advises.

Hydrangea paniculata 'Little Lamb'

Caryopteris × clandonensis 'Summer Sorbet'

Iris pallida 'Variegata'

"Plan the garden around your life. Don't plant a vegetable garden if you go to the cottage. Start planning around your rest spot. Consider not only where you will be sitting, but also think about the view from that spot. The view is what you want to be designing."

In his front garden in west Toronto, Paul put in a pathway that accommodated his family. "Ask, how does the mailman go from my house to the next? Create that path."

Paul suggests planting trees first to let them get established and start a canopy, put in hardscaping and then add evergreens, shrubs, perennials and annuals in that order.

For the sun garden he recommends these plants:

- Cedar (*Thuja occidentalis* 'Degroot's Spire')
- Variegated Japanese sedge (*Carex oshimensis* 'Evergold')
- Two-row stonecrop (*Sedum spurium* 'John Creech')
- Common sage (*Salvia officinalis* 'Berggarten')
- Variegated yucca (*Yucca filamentosa* 'Colour Guard')
- Bluebeard (*Caryopteris × clandonensis* 'Summer Sorbet')
- Variegated sweet iris (*Iris pallida* 'Variegata')
- Hydrangea (*Hydrangea paniculata* 'Little Lamb')
- Spurge (*Euphorbia* 'Diamond Frost')

Paul chooses the **cedar** for its form. It has a narrow columnar shape and slow-growing habit, with finely textured rich green leaves. Slow growing means less pruning.

The **variegated Japanese sedge** is often described as a grass and chosen for its year-round interest, as the clumps of green grass with golden edges still look good in January. Few pests attack the sedge; it divides easily, provides texture and only needs to be cut back in the spring. That haircut takes only minutes, according to Paul.

"Sage is a plant that always looks good. It has excellent silver foliage, which is really attractive from the time it emerges through late fall and early winter."

The **two-row stonecrop 'John Creech'** provides a tight green carpet with soft pink flowers in late spring through early summer. "There is nothing to do," says Paul. They are very compact and spread easily.

"**Sage** is a plant that always looks good," Paul explains. "It has excellent silver foliage, which is really attractive from the time it emerges through late fall and early winter. Put this plant near a pathway to enjoy its fragrance."

Variegated yucca 'Colour Guard' is considered one of the most dramatic variegated yuccas on the market. Its sword-shaped leaves have a golden-yellow central stripe against a green edge. In cool weather the yellow stripe turns rose-coloured. Branched clusters of creamy-white bells open midsummer on long stems.

Bluebeard is a favourite woody shrub. Its leaves, which emerge in late spring, are bright gold with green centres and are topped with bright blue flowers in the late summer and early fall.

"This is one of the few plants I grow only for its flowers," says Paul about the **variegated sweet iris**. "I love its fragrance and

❈ *Start small and add year after year.*
❈ *Design the view and the garden will follow.*
❈ *Plan the garden around your life.*
❈ *Put in paths that accommodate your routine.*
❈ *Plant trees first, then evergreens, shrubs, perennials and annuals in that order.*

- Father Hugo rose (*Rosa hugonis*)
- Japanese forest grass (*Hakonechloa macra*)
- Begonia – Mocha series, orange mocha

Paul likes the form of **greater wood rush**, a spiky mound that provides textural contrast in the garden. The foliage is all green and it shoots up brown spikes, he says. This robust sedge looks "stunning covered with snow," which is another reason Paul selects it.

Variegated yellow archangel is a spreading groundcover that is silver and green and turns burgundy in the fall. It is considered drought-tolerant and will thrive in just about any soil.

One of the most underused plants, Paul believes, is **red barrenwort** – and it is a workhorse. It is one of the few plants that can grow under maples. It provides interest mid-spring when it blooms with crimson flowers. Its semi-evergreen foliage turns red and then bronze in the winter. "I love the leaf shape," adds Paul.

contrasting foliage." This iris blooms late in the spring. Its leaves are strap-like with vertical striped ribbons of green, white and cream. The violet-blue flowers are held on the ends of 90- to 100-cm stalks.

Hydrangea 'Little Lamb' has the smallest leaves of any hydrangea, says Paul. It is space conscious and doesn't take up much room. Give it a hard cutting-back in spring and that's all you need to do. He particularly likes its green flowers. Even though hydrangeas do well in the shade, Paul feels that this one does even better in the sun.

"Epimedium is a workhorse. It is one of the few plants that can grow under maples."

Variegated broad-leafed sedge is another perennial that provides textural contrast. It has wide bright green leaves with distinct white stripes. The plant slowly spreads into clumps, excellent for either groundcover or edging.

The **Japanese kerria** is a shrub that requires minimum care. It has interesting stems that create a zigzag form. The flowers resemble buttercups, brightening the shade in the spring. A bonus is its bright green bark in the winter.

'Diamond Frost' spurge is a workhorse, which is why Paul included it, even though it is an annual. He adds that it is adaptable, needs no deadheading and has a long bloom of fine white flowers that last from late spring to hard frost.

For the shady garden Paul has chosen plants that are especially carefree:
- Greater wood rush (*Luzula sylvatica*)
- Variegated yellow Archangel, also known as dead nettle or false lamium (*Lamiastrum galeobdolon* 'Variegatum')
- Red barrenwort or Bishop's hat (*Epimedium × rubrum*)
- Variegated broad-leafed sedge (*Carex siderosticha* 'Variegata')
- Japanese kerria (*Kerria japonica*)

Paul is excited about **Father Hugo rose** for a host of reasons: it blooms in light shade, it has an airy arching form, and the soft yellow blooms are 5 cm wide and blossom profusely over the shrub. As well, the plant has smooth mahogany-coloured bark that contrasts with its finely textured green foliage. The foliage turns deep red in the fall, creating many seasons of interest.

The swaying of the **Japanese forest grass** in the wind is one of the highlights of this architectural plant. Paul is delighted by its rich green foliage and arching form.

This Master Gardener couldn't resist adding bright orange annuals to his shady garden to provide both colour and contrast. The **mocha orange begonia** has a vibrant and vivid orange colour over a rich brown foliage that works well with the green, yellow and cream flowers and the variety of colour and textures in this shade garden.

Paul Zammit, Director of Horticulture at the Toronto Botanical Garden, is one of the country's most popular lecturers. Find out why at www.torontobotanicalgarden.ca.

Hakonechloa macra 'All Gold'

The White Garden

Sonia Leslie has been involved with gardening since she was a child in England. During World War II everyone turned their lawns into vegetable gardens. She still grows vegetables in her exquisite North York, Ontario, garden. Vegetables and a bit of everything else. In fact, her garden is so densely planted that she doesn't have to weed.

"I have so many plants, bulbs and perennials that there is no room for weeds," she says. "If you have a good succession of plants and trees, weeds will not be a problem."

"I have so many plants, bulbs and perennials that there is no room for weeds."

As a Master Gardener, Sonia has many tips for building a low-maintenance garden: "It's worthwhile putting in a watering system. I have soaker hoses all over the garden that I leave in all year. Most perennials will survive if you never touch them, but you must water.

"Label your plants – use the labels from the nursery but have them deeply in the ground as frost will heave them out."

Sonia loves bulbs, not only because she considers them easy to grow, but also because they provide a thrill when the crocuses and snowdrops push their way through the snow in January.

"What I enjoy is having blooms from frost to frost."

Happily, she teaches us how to do that, with plants that will create a shimmering, glowing white garden. "But before planting," she advises, "find the best spot in your garden to sit. Build around that area with the sights, sounds and fragrances you enjoy."

Allium cristophii

❧ *Alliums are squirrel and deer resistant and last a long time in the garden.*

❧ *Choose mildew resistant varieties of perennials.*

❧ *Hostas with waxy or thick leaves are more slug resistant.*

Her plants for the sunny garden include these:

- Crocosmia (*Crocosmia × crocosmiiflora*)
- All alliums, but three in particular: Golden garlic alium (*Allium moly* 'Golden Garlic'); Giant allium (*Allium giganteum*); and Star of Persia allium (*Allium cristophii*)
- Striped squill (*Puschkinia scilloides*)
- Clustered bellflower (*Campanula glomerata*)
- Summer phlox (*Phlox paniculata* 'David' and 'Norah Leigh') – both are mildew resistant
- Japanese anemone (*Anemone* 'Honorine Jobert'*)*
- Hydrangea (*Hydrangea arborescens* 'Annabelle')
- Compact Lemoine deutzia (*Deutzia × lemoinei* 'Compacta')
- Boxwood (*Buxus microphylla* 'Green Mountain')
- Golden clematis (*Clematis tangutica*)

"White perennials go with anything."

Sonia explains the secret of success with bulbs is to plant them deeply. The **crocosmia** is very hardy with long pale green strap-like leaves, branching stems that grow in zigzag fashion. Its showy orange and yellow flowers spread to make sturdy clumps of colour in late August and September. Each flower is about 5 cm across and the nodding cluster can be several inches long. Crocosmia dies back to the ground in winter only to regrow from its circular, flattened corms in spring.

Another favourite is the **allium** – "any or all of them." These are members of the onion family, unappealing to squirrels or deer. Sonia assures us that you can't go wrong with any allium as they last a long time in the garden and then provide interest when they fade and dry. The three different varieties she recommends provide low, medium and tall heights and bloom from spring until midsummer.

Golden garlic allium is only 30 cm high and provides a cluster of bright yellow flowers in spring. The **giant allium** is a skyscraper, says Sonia, with deep lavender flowers. This huge purple flower can reach up to 15 cm in diameter and blooms from May to June. The **Star of Persia** variety blooms in midsummer and has a huge flower head with blooms spiking randomly. "It is the greatest fun," says Sonia. "It reminds me of the stars and planets."

The reliable **striped squill** blooms in early spring and easily can become a 15-cm blanket of blue in the garden or even throughout the lawn. (Warning: it can be invasive in some areas.)

The perennials Sonia selects are all long lasting, hardy and white.

Clustered bellflower blooms in midsummer to fall and often has two crops of colour. She recommends two varieties of **summer phlox**: **'David'**, which grows to 100 cm, and the 70-cm variegated **'Norah Leigh'** with creamy white flowers and a bright rose-pink eye. Both are mildew resistant and long lasting.

Japanese anemones wave their masses of white flowers on skinny stems throughout the late summer and fall. These reach a height of 120 cm and spread throughout the garden.

No white garden would be complete without a **hydrangea**, and the **'Annabelle'** variety has dramatic large glowing

Hydrangea anomala petiolaris

Japanese anemone 'Honorine Jobert'

Hosta sieboldiana 'Elegans'

globular heads that flower from midsummer until frost and then provide winter interest if left to dry on the stem. A perfect fit for a lazy gardener.

"White perennials go with anything," says Sonia. "When there is a lot of brilliant sunshine, colours don't show up as much. But when you go out in the evening, you can enjoy the glow of white flowers." In her garden, she combines white with reds and oranges. The most dramatic contrast, though, is with green shrubs and evergreens. She points out that the perennials listed provide bloom throughout most of the season, each picking up where the other left off. The evergreens provide interest all winter.

Sonia favours the fragrant **Compact Lemoine deutzia** for its white flowers in the spring. She recommends the reliable **boxwood** shrub as hedging, a natural barrier or a backdrop for the white perennials. Boxwood is a slow-growing plant, is neat and requires little maintenance or pruning.

Although Sonia had to restrain herself not to add more plants to the list, she insists that we include the climber **golden clematis**. Its flowers are bright yellow but it remains in the white palate because of its large white seed heads, which appear after it blooms. "In the fall, the sun catches the seed heads and they glow," says Sonia. This clematis climbs over her arbour, reaching almost four metres.

Although it is more difficult to have a white shade garden, Sonia balances the greens of her predominantly hosta and fern garden by using many plants with variegated white leaves.

These shady garden choices include the following:

- Hellebore (*Helleborus*) – all are wonderful
- Climbing hydrangea (*Hydrangea anomala petiolaris*)
- Japanese tassel fern (*Polystichum polyblepharum*)
- Lady fern (*Athyrium filix-femina*)
- Japanese painted fern (*Athyrium niponicum* 'Pictum')
- Autumn fern (*Dryopteris erythrosora*)
- Hosta – any but include the giant slow-growing variety (*Hosta sieboldiana* 'Elegans')

Hellebores are harbingers of spring. They have glossy deep green leaves and come in a wide assortment of coloured flowers. They spread slowly, creating a lovely groundcover throughout the season.

The **climbing hydrangea** can be grown against a wall, providing white flowers in midsummer over glossy large leaves. Although it is slow growing, the hydrangea is hardy and reliable in shade. A faster-growing alternative is the Japanese hydrangea vine (*Schizophragma hydrangeoides*).

The ferns grow into a sea of textures and shades of subtle colour. The Japanese **tassel fern** has lacy edging, while the **lady fern** has interesting fronds. The **Japanese painted fern** is a favourite because of its red veins, dark stems and silvery foliage. The beauty of the **autumn fern** is in its evergreen leaves and its bushy shape, although that fern also displays coppery-pink colour in its new growth.

The **hosta 'Elegans'** Sonia recommends has a true blue colour and large, heavily corrugated leaves, making it slug resistant. It produces white flowers in late June.

And Sonia's final piece of advice: "If you don't like the way a plant is doing, dig it up and give it away or throw it in the compost."

Master Gardener Sonia Leslie is involved in many aspects of the Toronto Botanical Garden and is a former member of its Board of Directors.

Gardening from a Hammock
with Susan Lipchak

A Tall, Dancing Garden

The cliché that when one door closes an-other opens resonates for Master Gardener Susan Lipchak. As a professional violist, she found herself without work in 1992 when the Toronto Symphony Orchestra lost its summer season at Ontario Place, Toronto. That opened the door to her large garden, and it inspired her to take courses and eventually get her Master Gardeners certification. Now, after 40 years with the symphony, she has retired and has even more time to garden.

Susan's large yard in North York is a "mix of things," with a woodland area, a rock garden, small pond, vegetable garden and sunny border. Her favourite plants are grasses, which are interspersed throughout with dramatic effect. Perhaps the music speaks through her because everywhere her garden is filled with tall, swaying and dancing grasses and perennials.

Susan considers herself a thrifty gardener. She suggests finding good bargains at nurseries and grocery stores at the end of the season, which is often the ideal time to plant perennials. She also participates in seed and plant exchanges. Yet she encourages people to spend money on structural plantings like shrubs and trees and on soil amendments. "Spend more on soil than on plants. If plants are sited correctly with good soil, they will thrive."

When it comes to plant selection, "I am not after the latest cultivar," explains Susan, and that is evident with her choices of old-fashioned, time-proven plants. "I like the idea of using natives because they attract birds and other pollinators."

For the sunny garden, Susan suggests these:
- Cushion spurge (*Euphorbia polychroma*)
- Purple coneflower (*Echinacea purpurea*)

The purple flowers of **Culver's root 'Fascination'** provide background spikes as they grow to a dramatic height of 120 to 180 cm. "I tend to like tall soldiers as this is a big yard and I like strong backdrops," says Susan.

Obedient plant fits that bill at 90 cm high. It stands straight in full sun with pink (native) or white (cultivar) blooms. "They can be somewhat invasive in a small space, although some of the cultivars are less so."

The two varieties of **goat's beard** also are effective; the *Aruncus dioicus* is a dramatically bold plant because of its size – it looks like a giant astilbe. It holds its own beside a giant clump of tall grasses in Susan's garden. This perennial stands 1.75 m and is spectacular in flower with

- Black-eyed Susan (*Rudbeckia fulgida* 'Goldsturm')
- Culver's root (*Veronicastrum virginicum* 'Fascination')
- Obedient plant (*Physostegia virginiana*)
- Giant goat's beard (*Aruncus dioicus*)
- Cutleaf goat's beard (*Aruncus dioicus* 'Kneiffii')
- Blazing star or gayfeather (*Liatris spicata*)
- Bachelor's button (*Centaurea montana*)

"I like using native plants because they attract birds and other pollinators."

Susan looks forward to her **cushion spurge** each spring. "I love it because when it emerges it is bright yellow with lime-green foliage and then it turns reddish in the fall."

Hybrids of echinacea are now available in a range of colours and flower shapes, but Susan prefers the tried and true native, the **purple coneflower**. Bees and butterflies are attracted to the flowers, and the seed heads are attractive to birds during the fall and winter. "The sight of snow capping the seed heads during the winter is an unexpected bonus," she says.

Echinacea purpurea

Black-eyed Susans are native, long-blooming and fairly drought tolerant. They also provide what Susan calls "a wow factor" in late summer and fall. These plants are easy to grow in just about any soil and spread to provide masses of colour. For lazy gardeners, make sure you plant them only where you want them to spread, Susan advises.

its creamy white plumes and lacy leaves. It eventually forms a dense clump. The **'Kneiffii'** variety is smaller, but still stands 90 cm and has finely cut leaves, which would suit a smaller garden.

The **blazing star** flowers from July through September and has tall, dense spikes of rosy-purple or white blooms. This follows the fringed blue flowers of **bachelor's button**, which blooms from June to July. The foliage is grey-green and grows in a mounding shape.

For the shady garden, Susan combines the following:
- Sweet woodruff (*Galium odoratum*)
- Hosta, any white/green variegation, but specifically (*Hosta* 'Undulata Albomarginata')
- Solomon's seal (*Polygonatum biflorum*)
- Japanese painted fern (*Athyrium niponicum* 'Pictum')

Galium odoratum

Aruncus dioicus

Hosta 'Undulata Albomarginata'

- 'Golden Shadows' pagoda dogwood (*Cornus alternifolia* 'Golden Shadows')
- Saskatoon serviceberry shrub (*Amelanchier alnifolia*)
- Lavender twist weeping redbud (*Cercis canadensis* 'Covey')
- Japanese spurge (*Pachysandra terminalis*)
- Bloodroot (*Sanguinaria canadensis*)
- Golden Japanese forest grass (*Hakonechloa macra* 'Aureola')

Sweet woodruff is a groundcover with fragrant dainty white flowers that bloom in early spring. "It was used as a herbal remedy to flavour May wine in medieval Europe," explains Susan. It picks up on the variegation of the **hosta** and the flower of the arching **Solomon's seal** and is a good background for the burgundy and silver foliage of the **Japanese painted fern.** The contrast of the Solomon's seal huge downward arc form, the upward reach of the fern and the mounding of the hosta add balance as well as texture to this interesting grouping.

The **'Golden Shadows' dogwood** is a cultivar of the native and adds interest and colour with its yellowish-green variegated leaf on horizontal branches. "They are bright golden leaves with a green splash down the middle," says Susan. The clusters of white flower bracts bring an additional dimension to this interesting tree.

The shrub she favours is the **Saskatoon serviceberry**, not just because of its white spring flowers but also because the berries make great pies or jams "if you can get them before the birds do."

The **lavender twist weeping redbud** is a favourite because it can be positioned under a larger tree, but it can also act as a specimen in the garden. It has a weeping form and produces lavender-pink flowers in the spring. Susan recommends planting groundcover beneath it, either sweet woodruff or **Japanese spurge**. The slow-growing Japanese spurge has glossy evergreen jagged leaves, and in the early spring white flowers appear.

"I love the **bloodroot**," says Susan, "especially the way it comes up with its little white flowers emerging from its

"The berries of the Saskatoon serviceberry make great pies or jams — if you can get them before the birds."

leaves wrapped around the stem." Its red root and red sap give it its name. It's an ephemeral, which means it will die back during the summer.

A lover of all grasses, Susan emphasizes that the **golden Japanese forest grass** is a must-have for the shade garden. It is low and clumping and cascades like a small waterfall of yellow-green variegated leaves.

Susan Lipchak is a Master Gardener who can be found volunteering at the Toronto Botanical Garden when not digging in her own yard. She is an active member of the Ontario Rock and Hardy Plant Society.

How to use the Botanical Reference Guide

This Botanical Reference Guide includes most of the plants recommended by our expert gardeners. It shows you what the plant looks like and gives you key information, such as:

- how tall and wide it grows
- how hardy it is
- details about its shape, leaves and flowers
- how to use it in your garden

We have used botanical names followed by the plant's common name because most nurseries will know the plant by its botanical name. If you need the common name to find your plant in this guide, please refer to the alphabetical listing of common and botanical names at the back of this book.

The height and spread of perennials are listed in centimeters and inches. Bigger shrubs and trees are in metres and feet. All measurements and hardiness zones are averages because growing conditions and your local microclimate will affect how a plant grows in your garden. It is always wise to check with your local nursery to confirm how a plant will do in your conditions.

It is important to note that all plants require full sun unless otherwise indicated under the "Uses" column.

Hardiness Zones

Hardiness zones for plants are an indication of the average winter temperatures in an area and can be used to determine if a plant is hardy or suitable for the winter conditions in your area. Select plants with a zone hardiness number the same or lower than your zone.

The hardiness zones for the plants in this book are indicated in the chart at the back and will also be printed on the label attached to each plant when you go to the nursery. Be sure to check with the nursery to see where the plant comes from and whether the label was printed in Canada or the United States. Most of the labels used in Canada are printed in the U.S. and may use U.S. hardiness zone numbers, which are different than those used in Canada. If in doubt, ask the staff at the nursery.

Note that other conditions can affect the overwintering of a plant in your area, for example, the depth of snow cover in winter, year-to-year weather variations, wind and microclimates around your house. A microclimate can be created by the protection from the wind caused by your house or trees, the warmth stored by brick or pavement, the amount of sun on your garden. All of these factors can affect the hardiness of plants in your garden.

For more information on Canadian plant hardiness zones, visit: *atlas.agr.gc.ca/agmaf/index_eng.html#context=phz-zrp_en*

Botanical Reference Guide

BOTANICAL NAME	COMMON NAME	HEIGHT	SPREAD	ZONE	DETAIL AND BLOOM TIME	USES
Acanthopanax sieboldianus or *Eleutherococcus sieboldianus*	Fiveleaf aralia	2.5 m (8 ft)	2.5 m (8 ft)	Zone 4–8	Arching, upright, thorny shrub with bright green foliage (tolerant of city pollution and dry shade)	• Barrier • Drought tolerant • Screening • Sun or shade • Thorns
Acer griseum	Paperbark maple	7 m (23 ft)	5 m (16 ft)	Zone 5	Oval-shaped tree with cinnamon-red bark that peels like birch and green leaves that turn bright reddish-orange in fall	• Accent • Specimen • Sun or part shade • Year-round interest
Acer palmatum 'Emperor 1'	Red-leafed Japanese maple	5 m (16 ft)	4 m (13 ft)	Zone 5	Vigorous, upright tree with ferny palm-shaped, purple-red leaves that turn scarlet red in fall	• Accent • Specimen • Sun or part shade
Aconitum carmichaelii 'Wilsonii'	Azure monkshood	1.5 m (5 ft)	45–60 cm (18–24 in)	Zone 3–9	Deep blue flowers curiously shaped like a monkshood on tall spikes early autumn	• Cut flower • Large borders • Late bloomer • Sun or part shade
Adiantum pedatum	Maidenhair fern	30–60 cm (12–24 in)	30–60 cm (12–24 in)	Zone 2–9	Rounded clump of delicate, fan-shaped fronds of light green lacy leaves on purple-black stems	• Accent • Edging • Part shade or shade • Woodland
Alchemilla mollis	Lady's mantle	30–45 cm (12–18 in)	45–60 cm (18–24 in)	Zone 2–9	Chartreuse flowers in June over a mound of scalloped, soft, green leaves that trap glistening rain drops (self-seeds)	• Accent • Cut flower • Edging • Groundcover • Sun or shade

	BOTANICAL NAME	COMMON NAME	HEIGHT	SPREAD	ZONE	DETAIL AND BLOOM TIME	USES
	Allium cristophii	Star of Persia	60 cm (24 in)	30 cm (12 in)	Zone 4–9	Huge globes of lilac-purple flower heads that bring fireworks to mind midsummer	• Accent • Attracts butterflies • Cut flower • Vertical interest
	Allium giganteum	Giant allium	90–120 cm (36–48 in)	25–30 cm (10–12 in)	Zone 4–9	Skyscraper with large rounded heads of mauve-purple flowers early summer	• Accent • Attracts butterflies • Cut flower • Vertical interest
	Allium moly 'Golden Garlic'	Golden garlic allium	30 cm (12 in)	15 cm (6 in)	Zone 3–9	Thick grass-like leaves with clusters of bright yellow flowers in spring (self-seeds)	• Attracts butterflies • Cut flower • Drought tolerant • Naturalizes
	Amelanchier alnifolia	Saskatoon serviceberry	2–3 m (6.5–10 ft)	2 m (6.5 ft)	Zone 1	White flowers on upright mounded small tree or shrub in May with delicious sweet, black-purple fruit and yellow and orange leaves in fall	• Fruit • Specimen • Sun or part shade
	Amelanchier x grandiflora 'Autumn Brilliance'	Serviceberry	7.5 m (24.5 ft)	5 m (16 ft)	Zone 4	Small tree or shrub with clusters of showy white flowers in May and reddish-orange fall colour	• Accent • Fruit • Specimen • Sun or part shade
	Amsonia tabernaemontana	Eastern blue star	60–90 cm (24–35 in)	75–90 cm (30–36 in)	Zone 3–9	Native star-like blue flowers on willow-like foliage in late spring-early summer that turns golden in fall	• Accent • Cut flower • Drought tolerant • Specimen • Sun or part shade
	Anemone x hybrida 'Honorine Jobert'	Japanese anemone	90–120 cm (36–48 in)	60–90 cm (24–35 in)	Zone 5–9	Tall, elegant, single white flowers with a yellow centre August–October	• Accent • Cut flowers • Part shade or sun • Vertical interest
	Aquilegia discolor	Alpine columbine	10–15 cm (3–6 in)	10–15 cm (3–6 in)	Zone 4–7	True dwarf alpine from the Pyrenees with soft blue and creamy-white short-spurred, nodding flowers in spring	• Accent • Rock garden or trough • Sun or part shade
	Armeria maritima 'Dusseldorf Pride'	Pink thrift	10–15 cm (3–6 in)	15–30 cm (6–12 in)	Zone 2–9	Evergreen, deep green foliage with deep-pink pompom flowers June–July (more if deadheaded)	• Accent • Drought tolerant • Edging • Rock garden or trough

BOTANICAL NAME	COMMON NAME	HEIGHT	SPREAD	ZONE	DETAIL AND BLOOM TIME	USES
Aruncus aethusifolius	Dwarf goat's beard	20–30 cm (8–12 in)	20–30 cm (8–12 in)	Zone 2–9	Creamy-white plumes early to midsummer on dwarf plant with fern-like, deeply cut leaves which turn red in autumn	• Accent • Cut flower • Edging • Part to full shade • Woodland
Aruncus dioicus	Giant goat's beard	120–180 cm (48–72 in)	90–150 cm (35–60 in)	Zone 2–9	Rather large plant with lacy leaves and a spectacular display of creamy-white flowers June–July	• Accent • Cut flower • Specimen • Sun or part shade • Woodland
Aruncus dioicus 'Kneiffii'	Cutleaf goat's beard	75–90 cm (30–36 in)	75–90 cm (30–36 in)	Zone 2–9	Finely cut leaves like a Japanese maple with creamy-white flowers June–July	• Accent • Cut flower • Specimen • Sun or part shade • Woodland
Asarum canadense	Canadian wild ginger	10–15 cm (3–6 in)	15–30 cm (6–12 in)	Zone 3–9	Native groundcover with heart-shaped, downy leaves and maroon flowers in May	• Edging • Groundcover • Shade • Woodland
Aster divaricatus	White wood aster	45–60 cm (18–24 in)	45–60 cm (18–24 in)	Zone 4–9	Native with tiny masses of star-like white flowers with yellow centres August–September	• Accent • Cut flower • Drought tolerant • Naturalizes • Sun or part shade • Woodland
Aster 'Little Carlow'	Aster	9–120 cm (36–48 in)	60 cm (24 in)	Zone 4–8	Bushy plant with blue daisy-like flowers with yellow centres late summer	• Accent • Attracts butterflies • Cut flower • Edging
Astilbe x *crispa* 'Lilliput'	Dwarf astilbe	15–20 cm (6–8 in)	20–30 cm (8–12 in)	Zone 4–8	Shiny cut leaves with salmon-pink flowers on airy plumes that move with the breeze July–September	• Edging • Part shade or sun • Rock garden or trough
Astilboides tabularis	Shieldleaf rodgersia	90–120 cm (36–48 in)	75–90 cm (30–36 in)	Zone 3–9	Giant clump of huge umbrella-like leaves with plumes of creamy-white flowers on giant stalks in July	• Accent • Part shade or sun • Specimen • Woodland
Astrantia major 'Ruby Wedding'	Masterwort	60–70 cm (24–28 in)	45–60 cm (18–24 in)	Zone 3–9	Dark green leaves with dark red star-like flowers June–August (may rebloom in fall)	• Accent • Cut flower • Sun or part shade • Woodland

	BOTANICAL NAME	COMMON NAME	HEIGHT	SPREAD	ZONE	DETAIL AND BLOOM TIME	USES
	Athyrium 'Ghost'	Ghost fern	60–90 cm (24–35 in)	30–45 cm (12–18 in)	Zone 4–9	Upright arching clump of unique ghostly, silver-gray triangular foliage	• Accent • Part shade or shade • Specimen • Woodland
	Athyrium filix-femina	Lady fern	30–60 cm (12–24 in)	60–70 cm (24–28 in)	Zone 3–9	Lacy-looking, bright green fronds form a dense mound for any shady corner	• Accent • Part shade or shade • Specimen • Woodland
	Athyrium niponicum 'Pictum'	Japanese painted fern	30–60 cm (12–24 in)	30–45 cm (12–18 in)	Zone 4–9	Compact clump of deep burgundy leaf stems with olive-green arching fronds lit with silver	• Accent • Edging • Part shade or shade • Specimen • Woodland
	Aubrieta pinardii	Rock cress	6 cm (2.5 in)	5 cm (2 in)	Zone 3–9	Gentle creeper with low mounds of deep green hairy foliage covered with pretty violet flowers in spring	• Edging • Rock garden and trough • Sun or part shade
	Belamcanda chinensis	Blackberry lily	75–80 cm (30-32 in)	60–90 cm (24–35 in)	Zone 5–9	Fan-shaped leaves with orchid-like orange flowers with red dots July–August	• Accent • Attracts butterflies • Cut flower • Sun or part shade
	Berberis thunbergii 'Rose Glow'	Japanese barberry	1.2 m (4 ft)	1.2 m (4 ft)	Zone 4	Rounded shrub with variegated rose-pink foliage mottled with dark red deepening to purple-rose tones in fall, with bright red berries fall–winter	• Barrier • Hedge • Thorns • Winter interest
	Brassica oleracea 'Red Bor'	Red Bor kale	100–120 cm (40-48 in)	100 cm (40 in)	Annual	Tall, frilled and curly deep purple leaves from late summer until hard frost (treat as annual but may self-seed)	• Accent • Specimen • Vertical interest
	Brunnera macrophylla 'Jack Frost'	Siberian bugloss	30–40 cm (12–16 in)	30–45 cm (12–18 in)	Zone 2–9	Clump of heart-shaped silver leaves with blue forget-me-not-like flowers mid–late spring	• Accent • Edging • Part shade or shade • Specimen • Woodland
	Brunnera macrophylla 'King's Ransom'	Siberian bugloss	30–40 cm (12–16 in)	30–40 cm (12–16 in)	Zone 3–8	Creamy, yellow-edged leaves with silver veins and blue flowers in spring	• Accent • Groundcover • Part shade or shade

BOTANICAL NAME	COMMON NAME	HEIGHT	SPREAD	ZONE	DETAIL AND BLOOM TIME	USES
Brunnera macrophylla 'Looking Glass'	Siberian bugloss	30–40 cm (12–16 in)	30–45 cm (12–18 in)	Zone 3–9	Sprays of cobalt-blue flowers in spring on heart-shaped, silvered leaves that fade to sterling as summer progresses	• Accent • Edging • Groundcover • Part shade or shade
Buddleia davidii 'Potter's Purple'	Butterfly bush	1.2 m (4 ft)	1 m (3.3 ft)	Zone 4	Dark purple flowers mid–late July until frost	• Attracts butterflies • Cut flower • Fragrant
Buxus microphylla 'Green Gem'	Boxwood	60–80 cm (24–32 in)	60–80 cm (24–32 in)	Zone 5	Small slow-growing rounded evergreen with small leaves	• Edging • Foundation • Hedge • Sun or part shade
Buxus microphylla 'Green Mound'	Little leaf or Green Mound boxwood	1 m (3.3 ft)	1 m (3.3 ft)	Zone 6	Slow-growing mounding evergreen with dark green leaves	• Hedge • Specimen
Buxus microphylla 'Green Mountain'	Boxwood	1.5 m (5 ft)	1 m (3.3 ft)	Zone 5	Upright dark green pyramidal evergreen with small leaves	• Foundation • Hedges • Sun or part shade
Campanula glomerata	Clustered bellflower	45 cm (18 in)	45 cm (18 in)	Zone 2–9	Large clusters of violet-purple flowers June–July	• Accent • Cut flower • Sun or part shade
Campanula rotundifolia	Blue bells of Scotland	25–30 cm (10–12 in)	20–30 cm (8–12 in)	Zone 2–9	Bright blue, bell-shaped flowers June–September	• Containers • Cut flower • Rock gardens • Shade or sun
Campanula rotundifolia 'White Gem'	White-flowered bellflower	30 cm (12 in)	25 cm (10 in)	Zone 2–7	Pure white bell-shaped flowers June–October	• Containers • Cut flower • Rock gardens • Sun or part shade
Carex elata 'Aurea'	Bowles' golden sedge	45–60 cm (18–24 in)	25–30 cm (10–12 in)	Zone 5–9	Upright chartreuse-yellow grassy foliage with thin green edge	• Accent • Edging • Specimen • Shade or sun

	BOTANICAL NAME	COMMON NAME	HEIGHT	SPREAD	ZONE	DETAIL AND BLOOM TIME	USES
43	*Carex morrowii* 'Ice Dance'	Creeping Japanese sedge	20–30 cm (8–12 in)	30–45 cm (12–18 in)	Zone 5–9	Slow spreading, grassy, arching, dark green leaves trimmed in bright white	• Accent • Edging • Groundcover • Part shade or shade • Woodland
44	*Carex oshimensis* 'Evergold'	Variegated Japanese sedge	15–20 cm (6–8 in)	20–30 cm (8–12 in)	Zone 5–9	Low cascading clump of dark green grassy leaves with a creamy-yellow centre	• Accent • Edging • Part shade or shade • Woodland
45	*Carex siderosticha* 'Variegata'	Variegated broad-leafed sedge	15–20 cm (6–8 in)	30–60 cm (12–24 in)	Zone 4–9	Striped, wide, green, grassy foliage with narrow white margin	• Accent • Edging • Groundcover • Shade • Woodland
46	*Caryopteris* x *clandonensis* 'Kew Blue'	Bluebeard	1.2 m (4 ft)	60–90 cm (24–35 in)	Zone 5–9	Intense dark blue flowers late August with oval, grey-green aromatic foliage	• Attracts butterflies • Drought tolerant • Fragrant
47	*Caryopteris* x *clandonensis* 'Summer Sorbet'	Bluebeard	80–95 cm (32–38 in)	80–95 cm (32–38 in)	Zone 6–9	Emerges late spring with bright gold leaves with green centres topped by bright blue flowers late summer–early fall	• Accent • Attracts butterflies • Cut flower • Drought tolerant • Fragrant • Specimen
48	*Centaurea montana*	Bachelor's button	30–60 cm (12–24 in)	30–60 cm (12–24 in)	Zone 2–9	Bushy clump of grey-green leaves with shaggy, blue flowers June–July	• Accent • Cut flower • Drought tolerant • Sun or part shade
49	*Cercis canadensis* 'Covey'	Lavender twist weeping redbud	2 m (6.5 ft)	2.5 m (8 ft)	Zone 6–9	Weeping form with heart-shaped leaves and lavender-pink flowers on the stems in spring before the leaves come out	• Accent • Specimen • Sun or part shade
50	*Chamaecyparis obtusa* "Fernspray Gold'	Gold cypress	2 m (6.5 ft)	1.5 m (5 ft)	Zone 4	Dramatic upright golden-tipped evergreen	• Accent • Specimen • Sun or part shade • Winter interest
51	*Chamaecyparis obtusa* 'Nana Lutea'	Hinoki false cypress	1.2 m (4 ft)	1.2 m (4 ft)	Zone 5	Dwarf pyramidal evergreen with gold-tipped leaves	• Accent • Specimen • Sun or part shade • Winter interest

BOTANICAL NAME	COMMON NAME	HEIGHT	SPREAD	ZONE	DETAIL AND BLOOM TIME	USES
Chamaecyparis obtusa 'Pygmaea Aurescens'	Compact bronze Hinoki cypress	1.2 m (4 ft)	1.5 m (5 ft)	Zone 4–8	Mounded evergreen with spreading branches of flat fan-shaped yellow-bronze foliage in spring, green in summer, rich coppery-bronze in winter	• Accent • Foundation • Specimen • Winter interest
Chamaecyparis pisifera 'Filifera Aurea Nana'	Golden dwarf threadleaf false cypress	1–2 m (3.3–6.5 ft)	1.2 m (4 ft)	Zone 4	Very slow-growing, dwarf, mounding, weeping plant with delicate golden threadlike foliage	• Accent • Specimen • Winter interest
Chasmanthium latifolium	Northern sea oats	80–100 cm (32–40 in)	45–60 cm (18–24 in)	Zone 5–9	Native with showy, drooping flowers and slender bamboo-like foliage that changes from green to copper in the fall then beige in winter (self-seeds)	• Accent • Cut flower • Drought tolerant • Edging • Sun or shade
Chelone lyonii 'Hot Lips'	Pink turtlehead	60–75 cm (24–30 in)	30 cm (12 in)	Zone 3–8	Shiny bronze-green leaves with pink tubular flowers that look like a turtle's head late summer–early fall	• Accent • Cut flower • Part shade or shade • Woodland
Chionanthus virginicus	Fringetree	7 m (23 ft)	7 m (23 ft)	Zone 4	Native large shrub or small tree with white frilly, panicles of fragrant flowers in May with dark green foliage turning golden in fall	• Accent • Fragrant • Screening • Specimen
Cimicifuga racemosa syn. *Actaea racemosa*	Bugbane	120–150 cm (48–60 in)	60–75 cm (24–30 in)	Zone 3–9	Tall spikes of creamy-white bottlebrush flowers above lacy green foliage August–September	• Accent • Fragrant • Specimen • Sun or part shade
Cimicifuga simplex syn. *Actaea simplex* 'Hillside Black Beauty'	Black snakeroot or Black bugbane	150–180 cm (60–72 in)	60–75 cm (24–30 in)	Zone 3–9	Arching spikes of fragrant pale-pink flowers above a clump of lacy purple-black foliage early fall	• Accent • Cut flower • Fragrant • Specimen • Sun or part shade
Clematis 'Durandii'	Clematis	1–2 m (3.3–6.5 ft)	1 m (3.3 ft)	Zone 4–9	Rambling non-clinging groundcover vine with 10-cm indigo-blue flowers July–October	• Cut flower • Fragrant • Long blooming • Vertical gardening
Clematis 'Etoile Violette'	Clematis	3 m (10 ft)	1 m (3.3 ft)	Zone 3–9	Vigorous bloomer with clouds of deep purple velvety flowers late June–July	• Fragrant • Long blooming • Vertical gardening

	BOTANICAL NAME	COMMON NAME	HEIGHT	SPREAD	ZONE	DETAIL AND BLOOM TIME	USES
	Clematis 'Guernsey Cream'	Clematis	2.5–3 m (8–10 ft)	1 m (3.3 ft)	Zone 4–9	Creamy-white flowers in late spring	• Cut flower • Sun or part shade • Vertical gardening
	Clematis tangutica	Golden clematis	3–4 m (10–13 ft)	60–90 cm (24–35 in)	Zone 2–9	Groundcover or climber (with support) with bright yellow bell-shaped flowers in summer followed by decorative white seedheads	• Accent • Drought tolerant • Groundcover or • Vertical gardening • Sun or part shade
	Clematis terniflora	Sweet autumn clematis	6 m (20 ft)	2 m (6.5 ft)	Zone 4–9	Twining vine with masses of scented white flowers August–October followed by silvery seedheads (self-seeds)	• Fragrant • Long blooming • Vertical gardening
	Clematis virginiana	Virgin's bower clematis	3–4 m (10–13 ft)	3–4 m (10–13 ft)	Zone 4–8	Native vine with sprays of fragrant white star-like flowers July–September followed by tufted white seedheads	• Fragrant • Vertical gardening • Sun or part shade
	Clematis viticella 'Betty Corning'	Clematis	2.4–3 m (8–10 ft)	2.4–3 m (8–10 ft)	Zone 4–9	Delicate, nodding, lavender-blue flowers late spring, early summer	• Fragrant • Long blooming • Sun or part shade • Woodland
	Coreopsis verticillata 'Moonbeam'	Tickseed	30–45 cm (12–18 in)	30–45 cm (12–18 in)	Zone 4–9	Buttery-yellow, daisy-like blooms on lacy foliage midsummer to frost	• Accent • Attracts butterflies • Cut flower • Drought tolerant
	Cornus alba 'Elegantissima'	Variegated red twig dogwood	2.5 m (8 ft)	2.5 m (8 ft)	Zone 3	Upright shrub with silver-edged delicate leaves and dark red winter twigs with blue-white berries	• Specimen • Sun to part shade • Winter interest
	Cornus alternifolia 'Golden Shadows'	'Golden Shadows' pagoda dogwood	5 m (16 ft)	2 m (6.5 ft)	Zone 4–9	Horizontal branching shrub with yellow-gold foliage with green at the centre of each leaf, white blooms early summer and black berries in fall	• Accent • Specimen • Part shade or shade
	Cornus kousa 'Satomi'	Kousa dogwood	8 m (26 ft)	8 m (26 ft)	Zone 5	Showy pink flowers in spring on dark green glossy leaves with red foliage and red berries in fall	• Accent • Fruit • Specimen • Sun or part shade

	BOTANICAL NAME	COMMON NAME	HEIGHT	SPREAD	ZONE	DETAIL AND BLOOM TIME	USES
	Cornus kousa 'Wolf Eyes' or 'Samaritan'	Kousa dogwood	3–8 m (10–26 ft)	5 m (16 ft)	Zone 5	Both have variegated foliage and slight leaf difference but the same white flowers late spring-early summer, and raspberry edible fruit and red fall colour into mid-November	• Accent • Fruit • Specimen • Sun or part shade
	Cornus mas 'Variegata'	Variegated cornelian cherry	6 m (20 ft)	5 m (16 ft)	Zone 4	Small tree with peeling bark, variegated foliage and yellow flowers in early spring, followed by red edible "cherries" August–fall	• Accent • Fruit • Specimen • Sun or part shade
	Cornus sericea 'Farrow'	Arctic Fire red osier dogwood	1.25 m (4 ft)	1.25 m (4 ft)	Zone 3	Dwarf, upright, multi-stemmed dogwood with bright red winter stems and white flowers May–June with burgundy leaves in fall	• Accent • Attracts butterflies • Sun or part shade • Winter interest
	Cotinus coggygria 'Royal Purple'	Smoke bush	4 m (13 ft)	4 m (13 ft)	Zone 5	Multi-stemmed bush with pink fuzzy airy puffs in summer on deep purple leaves that turn red in fall	• Accent • Drought tolerant • Hedge • Specimen
	Cotoneaster dammeri 'Coral Beauty'	Barberry cotoneaster	50 cm (20 in)	1.5 m (5 ft)	Zone 4	Arching branches with white flowers in spring, coral-pink berries summer–fall and red leaves in fall	• Groundcover • Sun or part shade • Year-round interest
	Crocosmia 'Lucifer'	Crocosmia or Montbretia	90–120 cm (36–48 in)	30–60 cm (12–24 in)	Zone 5–9	Clumps of deep green, sword-shaped leaves, with tall, arching spikes of brilliant flame-red flowers summer–fall	• Accent • Cut flower • Specimen
	Crocosmia x *crocosmiiflora*	Crocosmia or Montbretia	50–60 cm (20-24 in)	30–60 cm (12–24 in)	Zone 6–9	Forms dense clumps of pale green strap-like leaves with showy orange or yellow nodding flowers on slender, arching, zigzag spikes late summer	• Accent • Cut flower • Specimen • Sun or part shade
	Daphne mezereum var. *rubra*	Daphne	1.5 m (5 ft)	1.5 m (5 ft)	Zone 5	Mid-sized, upright shrub with fragrant, purple-red flowers, followed by toxic red berries late winter–early spring	• Accent • Fragrant • Sun or part shade • Winter interest
	Dendranthema 'Bolero' 'Samba' and 'Rhumba'	Hardy chrysanthemum	45 cm (18 in)	45 cm (18 in)	Zone 5–9	Daisy-like flowers late summer-early fall 'Bolero' – deep gold, 'Samba' – rose pink, 'Rhuma' – deep red buds open to coral-red blossoms	• Accent • Cut flower • Fall colour

BOTANICAL NAME	COMMON NAME	HEIGHT	SPREAD	ZONE	DETAIL AND BLOOM TIME	USES
Deutzia x *lemoinei* 'Compacta'	Compact Lemoine deutzia	1 m (3.3 ft)	1 m (3.3 ft)	Zone 5	Compact rounded shrub with fragrant white flowers early June	• Accent • Fragrant • Specimen • Sun or part shade
Dianthus alpinus	Alpine pinks	5–10 cm (2–4 in)	15–30 cm (6–12 in)	Zone 3–9	Grassy clumps of green leaves with large single pink flowers May–June	• Attracts butterflies • Drought tolerant • Fragrant • Rock garden or trough • Sun or part shade
Dicentra 'Burning Hearts'	Dwarf bleeding heart	25–30 cm (10–12 in)	30–45 cm (12–18 in)	Zone 3–9	Mounds of blue-grey, fern-like foliage with rose-red flowers mid-spring–frost	• Accent • Edging • Long blooming • Part shade
Dicentra 'Ivory Hearts'	Fern-leaved bleeding heart	30 cm (12 in)	30–40 cm (12–16 in)	Zone 3–9	Mounds of blue-grey, fern-like foliage with clusters of white flowers early summer–fall	• Accent • Edging • Focal point • Long blooming • Part shade
Dirca palustris	Leatherwood	1–2 m (3.3–6.5 ft)	1–2 m (3.3–6.5 ft)	Zone 4	Native rounded shrub with leathery bark and yellow flowers early May, yellow leaves in fall	• Fragrant • Part shade or shade
Draba norvegica	White whitlow grass or Norwegian whitlow grass	7–20 cm (3–8 in)	20 cm (8 in)	Zone 3–9	Native low evergreen mat of tiny white flowers March–April	• Drought tolerant • Rock garden or trough
Draba rigida var. *bryoides*	Whitlow grass	10 cm (4 in)	10–12 cm (4–5 in)	Zone 3–9	Cushion-forming bun of dark green, densely packed, minute leaves with yellow flowers March–April	• Drought tolerant • Rock garden or trough
Dryopteris erythrosora	Autumn fern	30–60 cm (12–24 in)	45–60 cm (18–24 in)	Zone 5–9	Dense mound with new fronds coppery-pink contrasting against older glossy green ones	• Accent • Edging • Part shade or shade • Woodland
Dryopteris 'Golden Mist'	Wood fern	50–60 cm (20-24 in)	60 cm (24 in)	Zone 5–8	Evergreen fern with smooth, glossy fronds opening golden orange in spring, changing to green by midsummer	• Foliage • Part shade or shade • Woodland

BOTANICAL NAME	COMMON NAME	HEIGHT	SPREAD	ZONE	DETAIL AND BLOOM TIME	USES
Echinacea purpurea	Purple coneflower	75–120 cm (30–48 in)	45–60 cm (18–24 in)	Zone 3–9	Native purple daisy-like flowers on coarse dark green leaves mid–late summer with seed heads for birds in winter	• Accent • Attracts butterflies • Cut flower • Drought tolerant • Long blooming
Echinacea purpurea 'Vintage Wine'	Purple coneflower	75–85 cm (30–33 in)	45–60 cm (18–24 in)	Zone 3–9	Large purple-red flowers with brown centre cone and non-drooping petals mid–late summer	• Accent • Attracts butterflies • Cut flower • Drought tolerant • Long blooming
Epimedium grandiflorum	Barrenwort or Bishop's hat	20–25 cm (8–10 in)	15–30 cm (6–12 in)	Zone 5–9	White flowers May–June on heart-shaped, bright green leaves tinged with pink that turn deep green with red veining, then bronzy in autumn	• Edging • Drought tolerant • Groundcover • Shade or part shade • Woodland
Epimedium x *perralchicum* 'Frohnleiten'	Barrenwort or Bishop's hat	25–30 cm (10–12 in)	15–30 cm (6–12 in)	Zone 4–9	Bushy, evergreen mound of green and bronze leaves with sprays of bright yellow flowers mid–late spring	• Edging • Drought tolerant • Groundcover • Shade or part shade • Woodland
Epimedium x *rubrum*	Red barrenwort or Bishop's hat	20–30 cm (8–12 in)	30–45 cm (12–18 in)	Zone 4–9	Cherry-red flowers on heart-shaped leaves that turn bronze with purple hues in fall	• Edging • Drought tolerant • Groundcover • Shade or part shade • Woodland
Epimedium x *versicolor* 'Sulphureum'	Yellow barrenwort or Bishop's hat	20–30 cm (8–12 in)	30–45 cm (12–18 in)	Zone 4–9	Creamy-yellow flowers on heart-shaped leaves in spring and leaves that turn green then dark red in fall	• Edging • Drought tolerant • Groundcover • Shade or part shade • Woodland
Epimedium x *youngianum* 'Niveum'	White barrenwort or Bishop's hat	20–30 cm (8–12 in)	30–45 cm (12–18 in)	Zone 4–9	Sprays of white flowers on bushy mounds of dark green leaves mid–late spring	• Edging • Drought tolerant • Groundcover • Shade or part shade • Woodland
Eryngium planum	Blue sea holly	90 cm (36 in)	45 cm (18 in)	Zone 4–9	Spiny grey-green leaves with steel-blue thistle-like flowers June–August	• Accent • Butterflies • Cut flower • Drought tolerant
Euonymus fortunei 'Kewensis'	Miniature wintercreeper	5–10 cm (2–4 in)	30–90 cm (12–36 in)cm	Zone 5–9	Trailing mat of tiny, leathery dark evergreen leaves similar to other euonymus but only 10 mm wide–15 mm long	• Edging • Groundcover • Rock garden • Sun or part shade

	BOTANICAL NAME	COMMON NAME	HEIGHT	SPREAD	ZONE	DETAIL AND BLOOM TIME	USES
	Euonymus fortunei 'Sarcoxie'	Wintercreeper euonymus	1.2 m (4 ft)	1.2–3 m (4–10 ft)	Zone 6–9	Upright, spreading evergreen with glossy dark green leaves with whitish veins and pinkish-white fruit in fall	• Groundcover • Hedge • Sun or shade
	Euonymus fortunei 'Sunspot'	Wintercreeper euonymus	1 m (3.3 ft)	1–2 m (3.3–6.5 ft)	Zone 6–9	Sprawling evergreen vine or upright mounded shrub with green-gold variegated leaves	• Groundcover • Hedge • Sun or shade
	Euphorbia amygdaloides var. *robbiae*	Leatherleaf spurge	30–60 cm (12–24 in)	60–75 cm (24–30 in)	Zone 6–9	Shiny, dark green leathery leaves with tiny green-yellow flowers late spring (good for dry shade)	• Accent • Drought tolerant Groundcover • Part shade or shade
	Euphorbia 'Diamond Frost'	Spurge	30–100 cm (12–40 in)	30–100 cm (12–40 in)	Annual	White flowers on frilly apple-green leaves late spring–frost (treat as annual)	• Containers • Groundcover • Long blooming • Part shade
	Euphorbia dulcis 'Chameleon'	Chameleon spurge	30–45 cm (12–18 in)	45–60 cm (18–24 in)	Zone 4–9	Dark purple leaves with greenish-yellow flowers late spring–early summer	• Accent • Edging • Specimen • Sun or part shade
	Euphorbia polychroma	Cushion spurge	30–45 cm (12–18 in)	45–60 cm (18–24 in)	Zone 2–9	Bright yellow flowers in spring on lime-green leaves that turn red in fall	• Accent • Containers • Drought tolerant • Edging
	Fagus sylvatica 'Dawyck Purple'	European beech	8 m (26 ft)	2 m (6.5 ft)	Zone 6	Narrow columnar tree with deep purple leaves that turn bronzy in fall	• Accent • Large screen • Specimen
	Fagus sylvatica 'Purple Fountain'	Weeping purple beech	4–6 m (13–20 ft)	4 m (13 ft)	Zone 6	Weeping form – with smooth grey bark and glossy burgundy leaves that turn green in spring and copper in fall	• Accent • Specimen
	Fothergilla gardenii	Dwarf fothergilla	90 cm (36 in)	90 cm (36 in)	Zone 6	Native shrub with showy spikes of fragrant creamy-white flowers in May with blue-green leaves that turn dramatic colours of orange, red and yellow in fall	• Accent • Fragrant • Sun or part shade • Woodland

BOTANICAL NAME	COMMON NAME	HEIGHT	SPREAD	ZONE	DETAIL AND BLOOM TIME	USES
Fothergilla major 'Mount Airy'	Fothergilla	1.5 m (5 ft)	1.5 m (5 ft)	Zone 6	Upright mounded shrub with fragrant white bottlebrush flowers in early spring and blue-green foliage that turns orange, red and yellow in fall	• Accent • Fragrant • Sun or part shade • Woodland
Fragaria vesca 'Lipstick'	Ornamental strawberry	10–15 cm (3–6 in)	30–90 cm (12–36 in)cm	Zone 2–9	Mound of green leaves with bright lipstick-red flowers and tasty fruit spring–autumn	• Edging • Rock gardens • Groundcover • Woodland
Gaillardia 'Oranges and Lemons'	Blanket flower	40–45 cm (16–18 in)	30–45 cm (12–18 in)	Zone 4–9	Profusion of daisy-like tangerine-orange flowers with yellow tips early summer–late fall	• Accent • Attracts butterflies • Cut flower • Drought tolerant • Long blooming
Galium odoratum	Sweet woodruff	20 cm (8 in)	30–60 cm (12–24 in)	Zone 3–9	Fast spreading low clumps of fragrant whorled leaves with star-like white flowers April–May	• Edging • Groundcover • Part shade or shade • Woodland
Geranium macrorrhizum	Bigroot cranesbill	25–30 cm (10–12 in)	45–60 cm (18–24 in)	Zone 2–9	Pink flowers on thick aromatic green leaves late spring with red leaves in fall (good for dry shade in tough locations)	• Accent • Drought tolerant • Groundcover • Part shade or shade • Woodland
Geranium macrorrhizum 'Ingwersen's Variety'	Bigroot cranesbill	25–30 cm (10–12 in)	45–60 cm (18–24 in)	Zone 2–9	Light pink flowers on spreading mound of thick aromatic green leaves late spring–early summer (good for dry shade in tough locations)	• Accent • Drought tolerant • Groundcover • Part shade or shade • Woodland
Geranium 'Rozanne'.	Cranesbill geranium	30–50 cm (12–20 in)	45–60 cm (18–24 in)	Zone 4–9	Sprawling plant with deeply cut green leaves and large violet-blue, cup-shaped flowers mid-June–late fall	• Accent • Edging • Groundcover • Long blooming • Sun or part shade
Geranium sanguineum var. *striatum*	Bloody cranesbill	15–20 cm (6–8 in)	45–60 cm (18–24 in)	Zone 3–9	Bushy mound of fine textured leaves that turn red in fall and soft pink flowers with crimson veins May–August	• Drought tolerant • Edging • Groundcover • Part shade or shade • Rock garden
Geranium x *cantabrigiense* 'Biokovo'	Dwarf cranesbill	15–20 cm (6–8 in)	30–45 cm (12–18 in)	Zone 4–9	Low spreading mat of evergreen leaves with white-pink flowers late spring–summer	• Drought tolerant • Edging • Groundcover • Long blooming • Sun or part shade

	BOTANICAL NAME	COMMON NAME	HEIGHT	SPREAD	ZONE	DETAIL AND BLOOM TIME	USES
115	*Geranium* x *cantabrigiense* 'Cambridge'	Dwarf cranesbill	15–20 cm (6–8 in)	30–45 cm (12–18 in)	Zone 4–9	Low spreading mat of evergreen leaves with bright magenta-pink flowers spring–late summer	• Drought tolerant • Edging • Groundcover • Long blooming • Sun or part shade
116	*Geum triflorum*	Prairie smoke	30–90 cm (12–36 in)cm	15–30 cm (6–12 in)	Zone 3–8	Native with ferny, cut leaves and clusters of nodding reddish-pink, flowers that burst into feathery pink seedhead May–June	• Drought tolerant • Groundcover
117	*Gillenia trifoliata*	Bowman's root	60–120 cm (24–48 in)	60–75 cm (24–30 in)	Zone 4–9	Native with airy, white, star-like flowers with red base and stems mid–late summer, red leaves in fall and long-lasting seedhead in winter	• Accent • Cut flower • Part shade or shade • Woodland
118	*Gleditsia triacanthos inermis*	Thornless honeylocust	20–30 m (65–100 ft)	20–30 m (65–100 ft)	Zone 4	Elegant ferny leaves that cast a dappled shade and turn yellow in fall with large twisted seed pods summer–fall	• Showy foliage • Specimen
119	*Gymnocladus dioica*	Kentucky coffeetree	17 m (55 ft)	13 m (42 ft)	Zone 5	Large compound leaves up to a metre in length with small pea-like fragrant flowers in May and 20cm seed pods in fall that can be messy	• Fragrant • Showy foliage • Specimen
120	*Hakonechloa macra*	Japanese forest grass	60 cm (24 in)	45–60 cm (18–24 in)	Zone 5–9	Cascading mound shape with slender arching green leaves like dwarf bamboo	• Accent • Edging • Part shade or shade • Woodland
121	*Hakonechloa macra* 'Aureola'	Golden Japanese forest grass	30–65 cm (12–26 in)	45–60 cm (18–24 in)	Zone 5–9	Cascading mound shape with slender arching yellow and green striped leaves like dwarf bamboo	• Accent • Edging • Part shade or shade • Woodland
122	*Hamamelis mollis* 'Pallida'	Chinese witchhazel	4 m (13 ft)	4 m (13 ft)	Zone 5	Sulphur-yellow, ribbon-like flowers in March and dark green foliage that turns orange and red in fall	• Fragrant • Specimen • Sun or part shade • Winter interest
123	*Hamamelis* x *intermedia* 'Arnold Promise'	Witchhazel	6 m (20 ft)	6 m (20 ft)	Zone 5	Fragrant bright yellow, ribbon-like flowers with reddish centers in February–March	• Fragrant • Specimen • Sun or part shade • Winter interest

BOTANICAL NAME	COMMON NAME	HEIGHT	SPREAD	ZONE	DETAIL AND BLOOM TIME	USES
Hedera helix	English ivy	10–15 cm (3–6 in) Can grow to 6 m long (20 ft)	60–90 cm (24–35 in)	Zone 5–9	Evergreen fast-growing vine with large glossy green triangular leaves and black berries in winter	• Groundcover • Shade or sun • Vertical gardening
Hedera helix 'Baltica'	Baltic Ivy	10–15 cm (3–6 in) Can grow to 6 m long (20 ft)	60 cm (24 in)	Zone 6–9	Evergreen fast-growing vine with medium size, dark green, triangular leaves that turn bronzy-red in winter	• Groundcover • Shade or sun • Vertical gardening
Helleborus x *hybridus* 'Ashwood Gold Finch'	Hellebore	45 cm (18 in)	45 cm (18 in)	Zone 5–9	Low mound of leathery evergreen leaves with golden-yellow flowers with strawberry-speckled centres, March–April	• Long blooming • Cut flower • Part shade or shade • Specimen • Woodland
Helleborus x *hybridus* 'Eco Dragon's Blood'	Hellebore	35–45 cm (14–18 in)	35–45 cm (14–18 in)	Zone 5–9	Low mound of leathery evergreen leaves with white flowers in late winter–early spring	• Accent • Cut flower • Part shade or shade • Specimen • Woodland
Helleborus x *hyrbridus* 'Maroon'	Hellebore	35–45 cm (14–18 in)	35–45 cm (14–18 in)	Zone 5–9	Low mound of leathery evergreen leaves with maroon flowers in spring	• Long blooming • Cut flower • Part shade or shade • Specimen • Woodland
Helleborus x *hybridus* 'Pink Veined' or 'Pink Stripe'	Hellebore	35–45 cm (14–18 in)	35–45 cm (14–18 in)	Zone 5–9	Low mound of leathery evergreen leaves with pink flowers March–April	• Long blooming • Cut flower • Part shade or shade • Specimen • Woodland
Helleborus x *hybridus* 'Royal Heritage'	Hellebore	40–60 cm (16–24 in)	45–60 cm (18–24 in)	Zone 4–9	Low mound of leathery evergreen leaves with nodding cup-shaped flowers in shades from white through pink, red, maroon and near black late winter–early spring	• Long blooming • Cut flower • Part shade or shade • Specimen • Woodland
Heptacodium miconioides	Seven-son flower tree	6 m (20 ft)	3 m (10 ft)	Zone 5	Upright tree with cinnamon peeling bark and creamy flowers late summer followed by green seed clusters that turn red then purple in fall	• Drought tolerant • Specimen • Sun or part shade
Heuchera 'Georgia Peach'	Coral Bells	35–75 cm (14–30 in)	45–60 cm (18–24 in)	Zone 4–9	Huge peach-coloured leaves with silver-white markings and white sprays of flowers June–August	• Accent • Edging • Specimen • Part shade or shade

BOTANICAL NAME	COMMON NAME	HEIGHT	SPREAD	ZONE	DETAIL AND BLOOM TIME	USES
Heuchera 'Hercules'	Coral bells	30–45 cm (12–18 in)	30–40 cm (12–16 in)	Zone 4–9	Marbled green and creamy-white leaves with stalks of scarlet flowers in June	• Accent • Edging • Specimen • Part shade or sun
Heuchera 'Lime Rickey'	Coral Bells	20–45 cm (8–18 in)	30–45 cm (12–18 in)	Zone 4–9	Evergreen mound with chartreuse, scalloped leaves and ivory flowers late spring–early summer	• Accent • Edging • Specimen • Part shade or shade
Heuchera 'Peach Flambé'	Coral bells	20–40 cm (8–16 in)	20–40 cm (8–16 in)	Zone 4–9	Ruffled peachy-orange and red leaves with tall stalks of tiny white flowers in June	• Accent • Edging • Specimen • Part shade or shade
Heuchera 'Plum Pudding'	Coral bells	20–65 cm (8–26 in)	45–60 cm (18–24 in)	Zone 4–9	Deep plum-purple leaves with a metallic finish and creamy-white flowers in June	• Accent • Edging • Part shade or shade • Specimen
Hosta 'Blue Angel'	Hosta	75–80 cm (30-32 in)	90–120 cm (36–48 in)	Zone 2–9	Large heart-shaped blue-green leaves with dense clusters of lilac-white flowers mid–late summer (slug resistant)	• Accent • Cut flower • Part shade or shade • Specimen
Hosta 'Fire and Ice'	Hosta	50–55 cm (20–22 in)	90–100 cm (36–40 in)	Zone 2–9	Variegated with a white centre and very dark green-blue margins on pointy leaves with lilac flowers mid–late summer	• Accent • Cut flower • Part shade or shade • Specimen
Hosta 'Great Expectations'	Hosta	50–70 cm (20–28 in)	75–120 cm (30–48 in)	Zone 2–9	Variegated, wide leaves with irregular blue-green margin and golden-yellow centre	• Accent • Cut flower • Part shade or shade • Specimen
Hosta 'June'	Hosta	30–40 cm (12–16 in)	75–90 cm (30–36 in)	Zone 2–9	Chartreuse-yellow leaves with streaky blue-green margins and lilac flowers midsummer (slug resistant)	• Accent • Cut flower • Part shade or shade • Specimen
Hosta 'Niagara Falls'	Hosta	70–75 cm (28–30 in)	90–120 cm (36–48 in)	Zone 2–9	Dark gray-green pointy leaves with a waxy sheen, heavy corrugation and pale violet flowers July	• Accent • Cut flower • Part shade or shade • Specimen

	BOTANICAL NAME	COMMON NAME	HEIGHT	SPREAD	ZONE	DETAIL AND BLOOM TIME	USES
142	*Hosta* 'Paul's Glory'	Hosta	55–65 cm (22–26 in)	90–120 cm (36–48 in)	Zone 2–9	Bright yellow leaves with wide blue-green margin and white flowers July	• Accent • Cut flower • Part shade • Specimen
143	*Hosta sieboldiana* 'Elegans'	Hosta	65–75 cm (26–30 in)	120–150 cm (48–60 in)	Zone 2–9	Large, true blue, heavily corrugated leaves with white flowers late June (slug resistant)	• Accent • Cut flower • Part shade or shade • Specimen
144	*Hosta* 'Sum and Substance'	Hosta	75–90 cm (30–36 in)	150–180 cm (60–72 in)	Zone 2–9	Large chartreuse-yellow leaves with a quilted texture and pale purple flowers July (slug resistant and sun tolerant)	• Accent • Cut flower • Sun or shade • Specimen
145	*Hosta* 'Undulata Albomarginata'	Hosta	40–45 cm (16–18 in)	80–100 cm (32–40 in)	Zone 2–9	Dark-green leaves streaked with lighter green and a wide creamy-white margin with lavender flowers July	• Accent • Cut flower • Part shade or shade • Specimen
146	*Hydrangea anomala petiolaris*	Climbing hydrangea	5 m (16 ft)	3 m (10 ft)	Zone 4	Slow-growing, climbing vine with showy lacecap flower heads midsummer	• Accent • Sun or shade • Vertical gardening
147	*Hydrangea arborescens* 'Annabelle'	Hydrangea	1.2 m (4 ft)	1.2 m (4 ft)	Zone 2	Creamy white, large snowball flowers midsummer, turning light green then drying to straw colour for winter interest	• Accent • Cut flower • Sun or shade • Specimen • Winter interest
148	*Hydrangea paniculata* 'Limelight'	Hydrangea	2.5 m (8 ft)	2.5 m (8 ft)	Zone 4	Large, upright panicles of flower heads that start out lime green, fading over the summer to white and finally brown in fall	• Accent • Cut flower • Sun or shade • Specimen • Winter interest
149	*Hydrangea paniculata* 'Little Lamb'	Hydrangea	2.5 m (8 ft)	2.5 m (8 ft)	Zone 3	Compact shrub with smaller panicles of white flowers midsummer into autumn	• Accent • Cut flower • Sun or shade • Specimen • Winter interest
150	*Hydrangea quercifolia*	Oak-leaved hydrangea	2 m (6.5 ft)	2 m (6.5 ft)	Zone 5	Upright, spreading shrub with loose panicles of white to pink flowers midsummer on large oak-leaf-shaped leaves that turn reddish-purple in fall	• Accent • Cut flower • Sun or shade • Specimen

	BOTANICAL NAME	COMMON NAME	HEIGHT	SPREAD	ZONE	DETAIL AND BLOOM TIME	USES
 151	*Hydrangea serrata* 'Preziosa'	Serrarata hydrangea	1.25 m (4 ft)	1.25 m (4 ft)	Zone 5	Red-brown stems with deep pink, lacecap flower heads late July deepening to reddish-purple in fall	• Accent • Cut flower • Sun or shade • Specimen
 152	*Ilex* x *meserveae* 'Blue Prince'	Blue holly (male)	2 m (6.5 ft)	2 m (6.5 ft)	Zone 5	Slow growing holly with typical spiny blue-green foliage; male doesn't produce fruit. Both male and female are needed to produce red berries on the female in fall and winter	• Accent • Hedge • Sun or part shade • Year-round interest
 153	*Ilex* x *meserveae* 'Blue Princess'	Blue holly (female)					
 154	*Imperata cylindrica* 'Red Baron'	Japanese blood grass	45–50 cm	30–45 cm (12–18 in)	Zone 5–9	Dramatic upright grass with deep red colouring becoming bright red in fall through frost	• Accent • Edging • Groundcover
 155	*Iris pallida* 'Variegata'	Variegated sweet iris	90–100 cm (36–40 in)	30–60 cm (12–24 in)	Zone 3–9	Violet-blue flowers late spring on contrasting strap-like leaves with stripes of green, white and cream	• Accent • Cut flower • Edging • Fragrant
 156	*Iris sibirica*	Siberian iris	60–100 cm	45–60 cm (18–24 in)	Zone 2–9	Grassy slender green leaves with delicate-looking flowers in shades of blue, rose, purple or white May–June	• Accent • Cut flower • Edging
 157	*Itea virginica* 'Henry's Garnet'	Virginia sweetspire	1.5 m (5 ft)	2 m (6.5 ft)	Zone 5	Arching shrub with 15-cm wand-like white flowers late June on semi-evergreen leaves that turn brilliant reddish-purple in fall	• Attracts butterflies • Edging • Sun or shade • Woodland
 158	*Juniperus horizontalis* 'Monber' (Icee Blue)	Icee Blue creeping juniper	10–30 cm	1.25–2.5 m	Zone 3–9	Compact ground-hugging evergreen with intense steely-blue foliage with purple-tinged tips all year	• Accent • Drought tolerant • Groundcover • Rock garden • Winter interest
 159	*Juniperus horizontalis* 'Plumosa Compacta'	Compact Andorra juniper	50 cm (20 in)	1.5 m (5 ft)	Zone 2–9	Compact, low, spreading evergreen with blue-green foliage that turns purplish in fall and winter	• Accent • Drought tolerant • Groundcover • Sun or part shade • Winter interest

BOTANICAL NAME	COMMON NAME	HEIGHT	SPREAD	ZONE	DETAIL AND BLOOM TIME	USES
Kerria japonica	Japanese kerria	1.5 m (5 ft)	2 m (6.5 ft)	Zone 5	Arching shrub with green stems and bright yellow flowers April–May but may rebloom off and on all summer	• Sun or part shade • Winter interest • Woodland
Kirengeshoma palmata	Yellow waxbells	90–120 cm (36–48 in)	75–90 cm (30–36 in)	Zone 5–9	Exotic-looking mound of maple-shaped leaves with late-blooming tubular yellow flowers August–September	• Accent • Cut flower • Part shade • Specimen • Woodland
Knautia macedonica	Crimson scabious	60–90 cm (24–35 in)	45–60 cm (18–24 in)	Zone 4–9	Bushy clump of grey-green leaves with pincushion, crimson-red flowers June–Sept	• Accent • Attracts butterflies • Cut flower • Drought tolerant
Lamiastrum galeobdolon 'Variegatum'	Variegated yellow archangel (also known as dead nettle)	20–30 cm (8–12 in)	90 cm (36 in)	Zone 2–9	Fast-growing green and silver variegated leaves with showy yellow flowers mid-spring and burgundy and silver fall colour. May be invasive in some areas	• Drought tolerant Groundcover • Part shade or shade
Lamium maculatum 'White Nancy'	Lamium	15–20 cm (6–8 in)	30–60 cm (12–24 in)	Zone 2–9	Fast-growing small silver leaves with green edge and white flowers spring–early fall	• Accent • Drought tolerant • Groundcover • Part shade or shade
Larix decidua 'Little Bogle'	Dwarf European larch	Up to 175 cm	60 cm (24 in)	Zone 3	Irregular, narrow shrub with short twisted branches and bright green new growth in spring, gold in autumn (slow-growing so may take 10 years to get to this 175 cm)	• Accent • Specimen
Lavandula angustifolia 'Munstead'	English lavender	30–40 cm (12–16 in)	30–60 cm (12–24 in)	Zone 4–9	Bushy evergreen with narrow, silver, needle-like, very fragrant leaves and lavender-blue flowers June–July	• Accent • Butterflies • Cut flower • Drought tolerant • Fragrant
Leontopodium alpinum	Edelweiss	15–20 cm (6–8 in)	20–30 cm (8–12 in)	Zone 2–9	Swiss Alps wildflower with silver-grey leaves and woolly white flowers June–July	• Drought tolerant • Edging • Rock garden or trough
Liatris spicata	Blazing star or Gayfeather	45–60 cm (18–24 in)	30–45 cm (12–18 in)	Zone 2–9	Native grassy clumps of leaves with spikes of rosy-purple flowers July– September	• Accent • Attracts butterflies • Cut flower • Drought tolerant

BOTANICAL NAME	COMMON NAME	HEIGHT	SPREAD	ZONE	DETAIL AND BLOOM TIME	USES
Ligularia dentata 'Desdemona'	Ligularia	90–120 cm (36–48 in)	80–90 cm (32–36 in)	Zone 3–9	Clump of large, rounded dark-green leaves with a purple underside and yellow daisy-like flowers July–Sept (needs moisture)	• Accent • Cut flower • Part shade or sun • Specimen • Woodland
Ligularia 'Little Rocket'	Ligularia	120–180 cm (48–72 in)	80–90 cm (32–36 in)	Zone 4–9	Clump of large, jagged, green leaves with purplish-black stems and spikes of yellow daisy-like flowers June–July (needs moisture)	• Accent • Cut flower • Part shade or sun • Specimen • Woodland
Luzula sylvatica	Greater wood rush	30–60 cm (12–24 in)	30–60 cm (12–24 in)	Zone 4–9	Low mound of grass-like, dark green leathery leaves with short spikes of green flowers in spring	• Accent • Drought tolerant • Edging • Groundcover • Part shade or shade
Malus 'Makamik'	Flowering Crabapple tree	13 m (42 ft)	13 m (42 ft)	Zone 2–9	Bronze-green foliage with large semi-double pink flowers with red long-lasting fruit in fall (may be messy)	• Accent • Fruit
Meconopsis cambrica	Welsh poppy	30 cm (12 in)	15 cm (6 in)	Zone 6	Deeply divided light green leaves with small yellow-orange flowers spring until early frost (self-seeds)	• Naturalizes • Part shade • Rock garden • Woodland
Miscanthus 'Purpurascens'	Flame grass	100–150 cm	60–100 cm	Zone 3–9	Upright clump of dark-green leaves with brilliant orange-red plumes in fall (does not self-seed)	• Accent • Cut flower • Part shade or shade • Specimen
Miscanthus sinensis 'Morning Light'	Maiden grass	120–180 cm (48–72 in)	80–90 cm (32–36 in)	Zone 5–9	Graceful, upright mound of narrow green leaves with creamy-white edges with coppery-pink plumes late fall (may be considered invasive in some provinces)	• Accent • Cut flower • Specimen • Sun or part shade
Monarda 'Aquarius'	Beebalm or Bergamot	90–120 cm (36–48 in)	60–75 cm (24–30 in)	Zone 3–9	Deep mauve to rosy-pink flowers on fragrant leaves July–September (mildew-resistant variety)	• Accent • Attracts butterflies • Cut flower • Fragrant • Sun or part shade
Myrrhis odorata	Sweet Cicely	90–120 cm (36–48 in)	75–90 cm	Zone 4–9	Native herb with bright green, lacy leaves and umbels of white flowers late spring–early summer	• Accent • Cut flower • Fragrant • Specimen • Sun or part shade

BOTANICAL NAME	COMMON NAME	HEIGHT	SPREAD	ZONE	DETAIL AND BLOOM TIME	USES
Oenothera missouriensis	Evening primrose or Ozark sundrop	15–30 cm (6–12 in)	25–30 cm (10–12 in)	Zone 4–9	Native large yellow flowers late spring–early summer followed by unusual winged seed pods	• Accent • Drought tolerant • Rock garden
Oxalis adenophylla	Chilean oxalis	15–20 cm (6–8 in)	7 cm	Zone 4–6	Rosy-pink flowers late spring on attractive, pleated blue-green leaves	• Accent • Rock garden
Pachysandra terminalis	Japanese spurge		15–20cm	15–30 cm (6–12 in) Zone 3–9	Evergreen groundcover with jagged glossy green leaves and white flowers early spring	• Drought tolerant • Edging • Groundcover • Part shade or shade
Paeonia 'Flame'	Single Peony		55–60 cm	60–75 cm (24–30 in) Zone 2–9	Long-lived perennial with scarlet-red petals and contrasting yellow centre early–mid-June	• Accent • Cut flower • Fragrant • Specimen
Paeonia mascula	Wild peony or Balkan peony	50–150 cm	60–100 cm	Zone 2–9	Deep rose flowers on attractive leaves in late spring followed by decorative seedhead	• Accent • Cut flower • Specimen
Paeonia suffruticosa	Tree peony hybrid	90–150 cm (35–60 in)	90–100 cm (36–40 in)	Zone 4–9	Large spectacular blooms in a variety of colours on woody stems with interesting foliage May–June	• Accent • Cut flower • Specimen • Part shade
Panicum virgatum 'Shenandoah'	Red switch grass	80–90 cm (32–36 in)	75–90 cm (30–36 in)	Zone 4–9	Upright clump of green leaves with distinctive red tips in summer, tiny reddish flowers in August and deep purple-red fall colour	• Accent • Drought tolerant • Naturalized garden • Specimen
Papaver orientale	Oriental poppy	45–60 cm	45–60 cm (18–24 in)	Zone 2–9	Various shades of red, orange, plum, or white satiny flowers late spring–summer on coarse leaves that disappear after plant flowers	• Accent • Cut flower • Specimen
Paxistima canbyi	Mountain Lover	30 cm (12 in)	60–90 cm (24–35 in)	Zone 2–9	Native, slow-growing, low, evergreen shrub with red flowers in May, bronze leaves in fall	• Edging • Groundcover • Rock garden • Sun or part shade

	BOTANICAL NAME	COMMON NAME	HEIGHT	SPREAD	ZONE	DETAIL AND BLOOM TIME	USES
	Pennisetum alopecuroides 'Hamelin' 187	Dwarf fountain grass	75–90 cm (30–36 in)	60–90 cm (24–35 in)	Zone 5–9	Upright mound of arching green leaves with spikes of silvery-white flowers that turn tan late August then golden in fall	• Accent • Cut flower • Drought tolerant • Specimen
	Perovskia atriplicifolia 'Filigran' 188	Russian sage	90–150 cm (35–60 in)	60–90 cm (24–35 in)	Zone 4–9	Upright clump of greyish leaves with spikes of violet-blue flowers July–October (works in poor, dry soil)	• Accent • Attracts butterflies • Cut flower • Drought tolerant • Fragrant
	Persicaria amplexicaulis 'Firetail' 189	Mountain fleeceflower	90–120 cm (36–48 in)	90–120 cm (36–48 in)	Zone 4–9	Tall, spreading clump of leathery green leaves with long spikes of deep red flowers late summer–fall	• Accent • Attracts butterflies • Cut flower • Groundcover
	Phlomis russeliana 190	Sticky Jerusalem sage	60–90 cm (24–35 in)	60–90 cm (24–35 in)	Zone 4–9	Grey-green leaves with whorls of yellow flowers late June–July with remarkable seedhead fall–winter	• Accent • Cut flower • Drought resistant
	Phlox paniculata 'David' 191	Summer phlox	90–100 cm (36–40 in)	60–75 cm (24–30 in)	Zone 3–9	Hydrangea-like cluster of white, fragrant flowers midsummer to early fall on dark green mildew-resistant leaves	• Accent • Attracts butterflies • Cut flower • Fragrant • Sun or part shade
	Phlox paniculata 'Norah Leigh' 192	Summer phlox	70–75 cm (28–30 in)	60–75 cm (24–30 in)	Zone 3–9	Hydrangea-like cluster of white, fragrant flowers with a bright rose-pink centre midsummer to early fall on green and white variegated leaves	• Accent • Attracts butterflies • Cut flower • Fragrant • Sun or part shade
	Phlox paniculata 'Shortwood' 193	Summer phlox	90–110 cm	75–90 cm (30–36 in)	Zone 3–9	Hydrangea-like cluster of bright pink fragrant flowers with a darker centre midsummer to early fall	• Accent • Attracts butterflies • Cut flower • Fragrant • Sun or part shade
	Phlox stolonifera 'Sherwood Purple' 194	Creeping woodland phlox	15–30 cm (6–12 in)	25–30 cm (10–12 in)	Zone 2–9	Native groundcover with evergreen foliage and showy clusters of fragrant purple flowers in spring	• Edging • Fragrant • Groundcover • Part shade
	Physocarpus opulifolious 'Coppertina' 195	Ninebark	2 m (6.5 ft)	2 m (6.5 ft)	Zone 2	Multi-stemmed, upright, spreading shrub with coppery-orange foliage and clusters of pink flowers with bright red seed capsules in fall (not susceptible to mildew)	• Accent • Drought tolerant • Sun or part shade

	BOTANICAL NAME	COMMON NAME	HEIGHT	SPREAD	ZONE	DETAIL AND BLOOM TIME	USES
	Physostegia virginiana	Obedient plant	90–100 cm (36–40 in)	60 cm (24 in)	Zone 2–8	Aggressive native wildflower with white or pink flowers that can be positioned on the stem July–early fall	• Attracts butterflies • Cut flower • Sun or part shade
	Picea abies 'Little Gem'	Norway Spruce	50 cm (20 in)	95 cm	Zone 3	Dense, slow-growing rounded dwarf evergreen with fine, lime-green foliage in spring that turns darker green	• Accent • Rock garden • Winter interest
	Picea omorika 'Nana'	Dwarf Serbian spruce	1.5 m (5 ft)	1.5 m (5 ft)	Zone 4	Dwarf upright evergreen ball with silver on the underside of glossy blue-green needles	• Accent • Rock garden • Winter interest
	Picea pungens 'Montgomery'	Blue Colorado spruce	1.5 m (5 ft)	1.25 m (4 ft)	Zone 2	Slow-growing dwarf conical evergreen with silvery-blue sharp needles	• Accent • Rock garden • Winter interest
	Pinus aristata	Bristlecone pine	2 m (6.5 ft)	1 m (3.3 ft)	Zone 2–9	Slow-growing small evergreen with white resin droplets on short dark green needles	• Accent • Drought tolerant • Rock garden • Winter interest
	Pinus cembra	Swiss stone pine	10 m	2.5 m (8 ft)	Zone 3	Slow-growing, narrow, columnar evergreen with dense foliage and green needles	• Accent • Drought tolerant • Specimen • Winter interest
	Pinus mugo var. *pumilio*	Mugo pine	1–2 m (3.3–6.5 ft)	2–2.25 m (6.5–7 ft)	Zone 2	Slow-growing rounded evergreen with dark green foliage	• Foundation • Hedge • Specimen • Winter interest
	Polygonatum biflorum	Solomon's seal	60–70 cm (24–28 in)	60–70 cm (24–28 in)	Zone 3–9	Native plant with white bell flowers hanging from arching graceful stems late spring with yellow colour in fall	• Accent • Cut flower • Part shade or shade • Woodland
	Polygonatum commutatum	Giant Solomon's seal	90–120 cm (36–48 in)	60–90 cm (24–35 in)	Zone 3–9	Taller native plant with white bell flowers hanging from arching graceful stems late spring with yellow colour in fall	• Accent • Cut flower • Part shade or shade • Woodland

BOTANICAL NAME	COMMON NAME	HEIGHT	SPREAD	ZONE	DETAIL AND BLOOM TIME	USES
Polygonatum odoratum 'Variegatum'	Variegated Japanese Solomon's seal	50–60 cm (20-24 in)	30–45 cm (12–18 in)	Zone 2–9	Arching stems of green leaves edged in white with white fragrant, dangling flowers in spring	• Accent • Cut flower • Fragrant • Part shade or shade • Woodland
Polystichum acrostichoides	Christmas fern	30–60 cm (12–24 in)	30–60 cm (12–24 in)	Zone 3–9	Tidy, medium clump of dark green leathery fronds remaining green all winter	• Accent • Edging • Groundcover • Part shade or shade • Woodland
Polystichum braunii	Braun's Holly fern	30–75 cm (12–30 in)	30–60 cm (12–24 in)	Zone 4–9	Clumping native fern, with thick, dark green ruffled fronds (evergreen in milder winters)	• Accent • Edging • Groundcover • Part shade or shade • Woodland
Polystichum polyblepharum	Japanese tassel fern	30–60 cm (12–24 in)	45–60 cm (18–24 in)	Zone 5–9	Arching, glossy green fronds with a tassel-like appearance as they emerge	• Accent • Edging • Groundcover • Part shade or shade • Woodland
Polystichum setiferum 'Herrenhausen'	Soft shield fern	50 cm (20 in)	60 cm (24 in)	Zone 6–9	Low mound of feathery, light green lance-shaped fronds (evergreen in milder winters)	• Accent • Edging • Groundcover • Part shade or shade • Woodland
Primula laurentiana 'Fernald'	Bird's-eye primrose	10 cm (4 in)	5–6 cm (2–2.5 in)	Zone 2–6	Native alpine perennial herb with lilac-coloured flowers on a long stalk 10–40 cm high late May–July	• Rock garden or trough • Sun or part shade
Pulsatilla vulgaris	Pasque flower	15–30 cm (6–12 in)	20–30 cm (8–12 in)	Zone 2–9	Fern-like foliage with crocus-like, lilac to violet-purple flowers followed by attractive soft feathery tufted seedhead March–April	• Accent • Cut flower • Drought tolerant • Rock garden • Sun or part shade
Puschkinia scilloides	Striped squill	15 cm (6 in)	10 cm (4 in)	Zone 4–9	Perennial bulbs with delicate blue-striped white flowers creating a blanket of colour in early spring (foliage dies back in early summer and bulbs go dormant)	• Naturalizes • Rock garden • Sun or part shade • Woodland
Pyrus calleryana 'Chanticleer'	Callery pear tree	13 m (42 ft)	5 m (16 ft)	Zone 4–9	Narrow columnar tree with masses of white blossoms with purple centers in spring, small yellow fruit and reddish-purple fall colour. May be invasive in some areas	• Accent • Fruit • Screen • Specimen • Vertical gardening

BOTANICAL NAME	COMMON NAME	HEIGHT	SPREAD	ZONE	DETAIL AND BLOOM TIME	USES
Rhododendron 'Northern Lights'	Azalea 'Northern Lights'	1–2.5 m (3.3–8 ft)	1.5 m (5 ft)	Zone 4	Variety of colourful fragrant flowers in spring: 'Northern Lights' (pink flowers, 2.5 m), 'Lemon Lights' (bright lemon-yellow flowers, 1.7 m), 'Pink Lights' (medium pink flowers, 2.5 m), 'Northern Hi-Lights' (creamy-white with yellow accented flowers, 1–1.5 m), 'Rosy Lights' (dark rosy-pink flowers, 1.5 m), all with purple leaves in fall	• Accent • Fragrant • Specimen • Sun or part shade • Woodland
Rhododendron 'Lemon Lights'						
Rhododendron 'Northern Hi-lights'						
Rhododendron 'Rosy Lights'						
Rosa 'Ballerina'	Hybrid musk rose	1.2 m (4 ft)	1.2 m (4 ft)	Zone 4–9	Elegant arching stems covered with sprays of fragrant, small, pink and white single roses June–October	• Accent • Attracts butterflies • Cut flower • Fragrant • Sun or part shade
Rosa 'Golden Gate'	Climbing rose	2 m (6.5 ft)	1 m (3.3 ft)	Zone 4–9	Clusters of 5 to 10 golden-yellow double flowers with citrus fragrance in summer	• Accent • Cut flower • Fragrant • Vertical gardening
Rosa hugonis	Father Hugo rose	1.75 m (6 ft)	2.25 m (7 ft)	Zone 5–9	Masses of 5 cm soft yellow blooms and smooth mahogany coloured bark on upright arching canes May–June	• Fragrant • Part shade or shade • Specimen
Rudbeckia fulgida 'Goldsturm'	Black-eyed Susan	60–75 cm (24–30 in)	45–60 cm (18–24 in)	Zone 3–9	Upright clumps of brown-eyed, golden-orange daisy-like flowers midsummer–fall with interesting seedheads in winter	• Accent • Attracts butterflies • Cut flower • Sun or part shade
Sagina subulata 'Aurea'	Scotch moss	1–2 cm (.5–.75 in)	15–30 cm (6–12 in)	Zone 3–9	Low evergreen moss-like lime-green groundcover with white star-like flowers midspring	• Groundcover • Edging • Rock garden

BOTANICAL NAME	COMMON NAME	HEIGHT	SPREAD	ZONE	DETAIL AND BLOOM TIME	USES
Salvia officinalis 'Berggarten'	Common sage	30–45 cm (12–18 in)	30–45 cm (12–18 in)	Zone 4–9	Low evergreen mound of grey-green leaves with violet-blue flower spikes early–midsummer	• Accent • Attracts butterflies • Culinary • Cut flower • Fragrant
Salvia x *sylvestris* 'May Night'	Salvia	40–60 cm (16–24 in)	40–60 cm (16–24 in)	Zone 3–9	Fragrant narrow leaves with purple stems and deep indigo spikes of flowers early June–July	• Accent • Attracts butterflies • Cut flower • Drought tolerant
Sambucus nigra 'Gerda'	Black Beauty elder	2.5 m (8 ft)	2.5 m (8 ft)	Zone 5	Purple-black, serrated leaves with contrasting pink fragrant flowers midsummer and dark purple berries early fall	• Accent • Attracts butterflies • Fragrant • Sun or part shade
Sambucus racemosa 'Sutherland Gold'	Sutherland Gold elder	3 m (10 ft)	3 m (10 ft)	Zone 4	Deeply cut, ferny golden leaves with fragrant creamy-white flowers mid-spring and red fruit early summer	• Accent • Attracts butterflies • Fragrant • Sun or part shade
Sanguinaria canadensis	Bloodroot	10–15 cm (3–6 in)	15–20 cm (6–8 in)	Zone 3–9	Native low clump of rounded, deeply notched leaves with white multi-petalled blooms April–May	• Accent • Edging • Part shade or shade • Woodland
Saxifraga tricuspidata	Prickly saxifrage or three-toothed saxifrage	15–25 cm (6–10 in)	25 cm (10 in)	Zone 1–8	Native low clump with reddish-tinged stems, leathery leaves and pale yellow flowers with bright yellow centres late spring	• Rock garden or trough
Schizachyrium scoparium 'The Blues'	Little bluestem grass	60–90 cm (24–35 in)	45–60 cm (18–24 in)	Zone 4–9	Native upright clump of blue-grey foliage with bronzy-orange colour in fall	• Accent • Cut flower • Drought tolerant
Sedum 'Autumn Joy'	Autumn Joy stonecrop	30–60 cm (12–24 in)	45–60 cm (18–24 in)	Zone 2–9	Mound of fleshy grey-green foliage and flat heads of dusty-pink flowers late summer, deepening to bronzy-red and then a rust colour in fall	• Accent • Attracts butterflies • Drought tolerant • Specimen • Sun or part shade
Sedum 'Jaws'	Stonecrop	30–60 cm (12–24 in)	45–60 cm (18–24 in)	Zone 2–9	Bushy mound of succulent blue-green, serrated leaves with bright pink flowers late summer–mid-fall and brown seedheads in winter	• Accent • Attracts butterflies • Cut flower • Drought tolerant

BOTANICAL NAME	COMMON NAME	HEIGHT	SPREAD	ZONE	DETAIL AND BLOOM TIME	USES
Sedum 'Postman's Pride'	Autumn stonecrop	45–60 cm (18–24 in)	45–60 cm (18–24 in)	Zone 3–9	Bushy mound of dark purple leaves with pink flowers in late summer followed by brown seedheads in winter	• Accent • Attracts butterflies • Drought tolerant • Specimen
Sedum 'Purple Emperor'	Stonecrop	30–40 cm (12–16 in)	45–60 cm (18–24 in)	Zone 2–9	Mound of rich purple-black leaves all season long with clusters of dusty-rose flowers late summer–fall (prefers poor soil)	• Accent • Attracts butterflies • Cut flower • Drought tolerant
Sedum 'Rosy Glow'	Stonecrop	20 cm (8 in)	30 cm (12 in)	Zone 2–9	Blue-green, low mounding fleshy foliage with ruby-red flowers mid–late summer (prefers poor soil)	• Edging • Drought tolerant • Groundcover
Sedum 'Vera Jameson'	Stonecrop	15–20 cm (6–8 in)	30–45 cm (12–18 in)	Zone 2–9	Non-spreading clump of mahogany-purple leaves with dusky-pink star-like flowers late summer (prefers poor soil)	• Attracts butterflies • Drought tolerant • Edging • Rock garden or trough
Sedum album 'Faro Form'	Baby tears stonecrop or Swedish stonecrop	1–2 cm (.5–.75 in)	20–30 cm (8–12 in)	Zone 2–9	Flat carpet of tiny, round light-green leaves, turning shades of red in summer and again in winter with white star-like flowers in summer	• Accent • Attracts butterflies • Drought tolerant • Edging • Groundcover • Sun or part shade
Sedum kamtschaticum	Russian stonecrop	10–15 cm (3–6 in)	30–60 cm (12–24 in)	Zone 2–9	Low carpet of scalloped green leaves with bright yellow star-like flowers in June	• Accent • Attracts butterflies • Drought tolerant • Edging • Groundcover • Sun or part shade
Sedum kamtschaticum 'Weihenstephaner Gold'	Russian stonecrop	7–12 cm (3–5 in)	30–60 cm (12–24 in)	Zone 2–9	Low carpet of scalloped green leaves with coppery stems and clusters of golden-yellow star-like flowers in June and red foliage in fall	• Accent • Attracts butterflies • Drought tolerant • Edging • Groundcover • Sun or part shade
Sedum reflexum 'Blue Spruce'	Stonecrop	15–20 cm (6–8 in)	30–60 cm (12–24 in)	Zone 2–9	Narrow fleshy needle-like, blue-green foliage with clusters of bright yellow star-like flowers midsummer	• Accent • Attracts butterflies • Drought tolerant • Edging • Groundcover

BOTANICAL NAME	COMMON NAME	HEIGHT	SPREAD	ZONE	DETAIL AND BLOOM TIME	USES
Sedum rupestre 'Angelina'	Angelina stonecrop or stone orpine stonecrop	10–15 cm (3–6 in)	30–60 cm (12–24 in)	Zone 3–9	Trailing mat of succulent golden-yellow leaves with clusters of yellow star-like flowers in summer	• Accent • Attracts butterflies • Drought tolerant • Edging • Groundcover • Sun or part shade
Sedum sieboldii	October Daphne or stonecrop	15–25 cm (6–10 in)	30–45 cm (12–18 in)	Zone 4–9	Cascading mound of succulent grey-green leaves edged with red with clusters of soft-pink flowers late August–end of October	• Accent • Attracts butterflies • Drought tolerant • Edging • Groundcover • Sun or part shade
Sedum spectabile 'Brilliant'	Showy stonecrop	45–60 cm (18–24 in)	45–60 cm (18–24 in)	Zone 2–9	Thick green leaves with enormous mauve-pink flower heads that turn rich rusty-red summer–fall	• Accent • Attracts butterflies • Cut flower • Drought tolerant • Specimen • Sun or part shade
Sedum spurium 'Dragon's Blood'	Two-row stonecrop	10–15 cm (3–6 in)	30–60 cm (12–24 in)	Zone 2–9	Fast-growing, low carpet of small, bronzy green to beet-red leaves with clusters of ruby-red star-like flowers early–late summer	• Accent • Attracts butterflies • Drought tolerant • Edging • Sun or part shade
Sedum spurium 'John Creech'	Two-row stonecrop	5–10 cm (2–4 in)	25–30 cm (10–12 in)	Zone 2–9	Very low mat of rounded deep-green leaves with small clusters of mauve-pink star-like flowers in summer	• Accent • Attracts butterflies • Drought tolerant • Edging • Sun or part shade
Sedum spurium 'Red Carpet'	Two-row stonecrop	5–10 cm (2–4 in)	25–30 cm (10–12 in)	Zone 2–9	Carmine-red flowers late summer on red-tinged foliage that turns deep burgundy in fall and winter	• Accent • Attracts butterflies • Drought tolerant • Edging • Sun or part shade
Sedum spurium 'Voodoo'	Two-row stonecrop	10–15 cm (3–6 in)	30–60 cm (12–24 in)	Zone 2–9	Spreading mat of deep-red succulent leaves with clusters of tiny rose-pink flowers in summer	• Accent • Attracts butterflies • Drought tolerant • Edging • Sun or part shade
Sedum telephium 'Matrona'	Autumn stonecrop	40–50 cm (16–20 in)	45–60 cm (18–24 in)	Zone 3–9	Tall plant with grey-green leaves edged with pink and large clusters of soft pink flowers late summer–fall	• Accent • Attracts butterflies • Cut flower • Drought tolerant • Specimen

	BOTANICAL NAME	COMMON NAME	HEIGHT	SPREAD	ZONE	DETAIL AND BLOOM TIME	USES
248	*Solidago flexicaulis* 'Variegata'	Variegated zigzag goldenrod	45–60 cm (18–24 in)	45–60 cm (18–24 in)	Zone 3–8	Large pointy green leaves, edged with chartreuse and gold in early summer with yellow flowers early September–mid-October	• Accent • Attracts butterflies • Part shade or sun • Woodland
249	*Solidago rugosa* 'Fireworks'	Goldenrod	90–120 cm (36–48 in)	60–75 cm (24–30 in)	Zone 4–9	Bushy, upright clump of dark-green leaves with golden-yellow flowers like streaming yellow fireworks late summer–mid-fall	• Accent • Attracts butterflies • Cut flower • Specimen • Sun or part shade
250	*Spirea* x *bumalda* 'Goldflame'	Spirea	1 m (3.3 ft)	1.25 m (4 ft)	Zone 2	Dwarf shrub with burnt-orange leaves that turn green in summer then flame colour in fall with hot pink flowers in July	• Accent • Attracts butterflies • Cut flower
251	*Sporobolus heterolepis*	Prairie dropseed	70–75 cm (28–30 in)	45–60 cm (18–24 in)	Zone 4–9	Native clumping grass with flowing hair-like green leaves and fragrant silvery flower panicles late summer changing to orange and tan in fall	• Accent • Drought tolerant • Fragrant • Groundcover • Specimen • Sun or part shade
252	*Stachys monieri* 'Hummelo'	Alpine betony	45–50 cm (18–20 in)	45–60 cm (18–24 in)	Zone 4–9	Low mound of puckered, apple-green foliage with tall stalks of spiky pink flowers midsummer–fall	• Accent • Attracts bees • Cut flower
253	*Stylophorum diphyllum*	Wood poppy	30–45 cm (12–18 in)	30–45 cm (12–18 in)	Zone 4	Buttery-yellow flowers in May with irregularly lobed leaves look good with woodland phlox or Virginia bluebells	• Edging • Part shade or shade • Woodland
254	*Syringa* 'Bloomerang'	Dwarf lilac	1.2–1.5 m (4–5 ft)	1.2 m (4 ft)	Zone 4	Small repeat-blooming shrub with fragrant purple-pink flowers spring–fall (heavier bloom in the spring; remove spent blooms to encourage reblooming)	• Accent • Attracts butterflies • Drought tolerant • Fragrant • Hedge
255	*Syringa vulgaris* 'Krasavitsa Moskvy'	'Beauty of Moscow' lilac	3.5 m (11 ft)	2.5 m (8 ft)	Zone 4	Bushy upright shrub with large, fragrant, double, white flowers with a tinge of pink in spring	• Accent • Attracts butterflies • Cut flower • Fragrant • Sun or part shade
256	*Taxus cuspidata* 'Capitata'	Japanese pyramidal yew	2.5 m (8 ft)	2 m (6.5 ft)	Zone 4	Dense, pyramidal evergreen with dark green needles and red fruit in winter	• Accent • Specimen • Sun or shade • Vertical interest • Winter interest

	BOTANICAL NAME	COMMON NAME	HEIGHT	SPREAD	ZONE	DETAIL AND BLOOM TIME	USES
257	*Thalictrum rochebruneanum* 'Lavender Mist'	Meadowrue	150–180 cm (60–72 in)	45–60 cm (18–24 in)	Zone 4–9	Lacy green foliage and tall purple stems with delicate purple flowers July–August	• Accent • Cut flower • Part shade • Specimen • Woodland
258	*Thuja occidentalis* 'Degroot's Spire'	Cedar	3–5 m (10–16 ft)	50–75 cm (20–30 in)	Zone 3–9	Pencil-thin, slow-growing columnar evergreen with medium green, finely textured foliage	• Accent • Sun or part shade • Vertical interest • Winter interest
259	*Thymus serpyllum* 'Pink Chintz'	Creeping thyme, Mother-of-thyme	5–10 cm (2–4 in)	30–60 cm (12–24 in)	Zone 2–9	Flat-growing mat of fragrant fuzzy green leaves covered in pink flowers in spring	• Accent • Attracts butterflies • Drought tolerant • Fragrant • Rock garden or trough
260	*Tiarella* 'Iron Butterfly'	Foamflower	20–40 cm (8–16 in)	25–30 cm (10–12 in)	Zone 4–9	Large, deeply cut leaves, edged in dark green with a purple-black centre and delicate spikes of fragrant, soft-pink flowers late spring–summer	• Accent • Edging • Fragrant • Part shade or shade • Woodland
261	*Tigridia*	Tiger flower	45–60 cm (18–24 in)	7–15 cm (3–6 in)	Zone 7	Tender Mexican bulb with 15-cm blooms end of July–frost in a variety of flashy colours (treat as annual)	• Accent • Containers • Cut flower
262	*Tricyrtis hirta*	Toad lily	60–90 cm (24–35 in)	45–60 cm (18–24 in)	Zone 4–9	Leafy, arching stems with bizarre star-like flowers, often marked with spots of dark purple late summer–fall	• Accent • Cut flower • Part shade or shade • Specimen • Woodland
263	*Tricyrtis hirta* 'Miyazaki'	Toad lily	45–60 cm (18–24 in)	45–60 cm (18–24 in)	Zone 4–9	Attractive green mound with starfish-like pale mauve and purple spotted flowers late summer–fall	• Accent • Cut flower • Part shade or shade • Specimen • Woodland
264	*Tsuga canadensis*	Canadian hemlock	20 m (65 ft)	5 m (16 ft)	Zone 4	Native pyramidal evergreen with soft yellow-green foliage in spring that turns glossy dark green	• Accent • Screening • Sun or shade • Vertical gardening
265	*Tsuga canadensis* 'Curly'	Canadian hemlock	10 cm (4 in) (in trough)	30 cm (12 in) (in trough)	Zone 5 (in trough)	Dwarf, irregular evergreen with a weeping form and needles that curl part way around the stems	• Accent • Specimen • Sun or part shade • Rock garden or trough

BOTANICAL NAME	COMMON NAME	HEIGHT	SPREAD	ZONE	DETAIL AND BLOOM TIME	USES
Tsuga canadensis 'Jeddeloh'	Dwarf Canadian hemlock	1.2 m (4 ft)	1.5 m (5 ft)	Zone 4	Slow-growing, graceful, evergreen fine-textured mound with emerald green needles	• Accent • Rock garden • Sun or shade • Winter interest
Tulipa clusiana 'Lady Jane'	Species tulip	20–25 cm (8–10 in)	15 cm (6 in)	Zone 4-8	Thin grey-green foliage with bowl-shaped white flowers with pink stripes late spring–early summer	• Accent • Edging • Naturalizes • Rock garden
Tulipa tarda	Species tulip	15 cm (6 in)	15 cm (6 in)	Zone 4–8	Recurved, shiny green leaves with 4 to 6 star-like, yellow flowers with white feathering on the edges early spring	• Accent • Edging • Naturalizes • Rock garden
Tulipa turkestanica	Species tulip	10–15 cm (3–6 in)	15 cm (6 in)	Zone 3–8	Star-like white flowers with a yellow centre; each bulb with 1 to 12 flowers early spring	• Accent • Edging • Naturalizes • Rock garden
Verbena bonariensis	Brazilian verbena	90–120 cm (36–48 in)	30–60 cm (12–24 in)	Zone 7–9	Upright branching stems with clusters of purple flowers that act like a veil in the garden early summer–late fall	• Accent • Attracts butterflies • Cut flower • Drought tolerant
Veronica 'Sunny Border Blue'	Speedwell	30–45 cm (12–18 in)	30–45 cm (12–18 in)	Zone 3–9	Bushy clump of crinkled, dark-green leaves with spikes of deep violet-blue flowers summer–fall	• Accent • Attracts butterflies • Cut flower • Edging • Sun or part shade
Veronica spicata 'Red Fox'	Spike Speedwell	30–45 cm (12–18 in)	30–45 cm (12–18 in)	Zone 2–9	Bushy clump of crinkled, dark-green leaves with magenta-red spikes June–late summer	• Accent • Attracts butterflies • Cut flower • Edging • Sun or part shade
Veronicastrum virginicum	Culver's root	120–180 cm (48–72 in)	75–90 cm (30–36 in)	Zone 3–9	Tall, native bushy clump of dark-green whorled leaves with elegant spikes of white flowers late summer–fall	• Accent • Attracts butterflies • Cut flower • Specimen • Vertical interest
Veronicastrum virginicum 'Fascination'	Culver's root	120–180 cm (48–72 in)	45–60 cm (18–24 in)	Zone 3–9	Tall bushy clump of dark-green, red tinged, whorled leaves with elegant spikes of purple flowers July–August	• Accent • Attracts butterflies • Cut flower • Specimen • Sun or part shade • Vertical interest

BOTANICAL NAME	COMMON NAME	HEIGHT	SPREAD	ZONE	DETAIL AND BLOOM TIME	USES
Viburnum carlesii	Koreanspice viburnum	1.5 m (5 ft)	1.5 m (5 ft)	Zone 4	Upright shrub covered with sweet-smelling ball-shaped clusters of pinkish-white flowers in early spring followed by red leaves in fall	• Accent • Fragrant • Specimen • Sun or part shade
Viburnum farreri 'Nanum'	Dwarf fragrant viburnum	1 m (3.3 ft)	1.2 m (4 ft)	Zone 6	Dense, compact, mounding shrub with pinkish-white flowers in early spring followed by deep purple leaves and black fruit in fall	• Accent • Fragrant • Fruit • Specimen • Sun or part shade
Viburnum plicatum f. *tomentosum* 'Mariesii'	Doublefile viburnum	2.5 m (8 ft)	2.5 m (8 ft)	Zone 5	Multi-stemmed, rounded shrub with horizontal branches covered in white lacecap flowers in mid-spring, red fruit late summer and brick-red leaves in fall	• Accent • Attracts birds • Fruit • Specimen • Sun or part shade
Viburnum trilobum	Highbush cranberry	3 m (10 ft)	3 m (10 ft)	Zone 2	Clusters of dainty white flowers late June followed by cranberry-sized, bright red fruit August throughout winter and fiery red leaves in fall	• Accent • Fruit • Screening • Specimen • Sun or part shade
Viburnum x *carlcephalum*	Fragrant viburnum	2 m (6.5 ft)	2 m (6.5 ft)	Zone 6–9	Upright, rounded shrub with pink flower buds followed by very fragrant white flowers in spring and purple leaves in fall	• Accent • Fragrant • Screening • Sun or part shade
Vinca minor	Periwinkle	10–15 cm (4–6 in)	60–90 cm (24–35 in)	Zone 3–9	Dense mat of glossy dark leaves with bright purple spring flowers (grows rapidly in moist soil, slowly in dry soil). May be invasive in some areas	• Accent • Drought tolerant • Edging • Groundcover • Part shade or shade
Vinca minor 'Illumination'	Variegated periwinkle	10–15 cm (4–6 in)	60–90 cm (24–35 in)	Zone 4–9	Golden-yellow leaves edged in green with blue flowers in spring (less vigorous than *Vinca minor*)	• Accent • Drought tolerant • Edging • Groundcover • Part shade or shade
Yucca filamentosa 'Colour Guard'	Variegated yucca	90–150 cm (35–60 in)	75–90 cm (30–36 in)	Zone 4–9	Evergreen, leathery, sword-shaped, grey-green leaves with a buttery-yellow centre and clusters of creamy-white bells midsummer	• Accent • Cut flower • Drought tolerant • Specimen
Yucca filifera 'Golden Sword'	Golden sword yucca	90–150 cm (35–60 in)	75–100 cm	Zone 4–9	Evergreen, sword-shaped gold leaves with dark green stripe and spikes of white flowers in summer	• Accent • Cut flower • Drought tolerant • Specimen

Index of Plants by Botanical and Common Name

Special Thank You to our Photo Suppliers

We would like to thank the following organizations and individuals for generously allowing us to use their photos in this book. Without them you would not be able to enjoy fully the beauty of the plants that have been recommended by our experts.

Bailey Nurseries, Inc.
www.baileynurseries.com

Walter Blonski, photographer

Dugald Cameron, Garden Import

Connon Nurseries *www.connon.ca*

Dan Cooper, Master Gardener and photographer
www.istockphoto.com/coopermoisse

Marilyn Cornwell, artist and photographer *www.marilyncornwell.com/-/marilyncornwell*

Lorraine Flanigan, editor, writer and blogger *citygardeningonline.com*

Belinda Gallagher, Hooked on Horticulture *www.hookedonhorticulture.com.*

Heritage Perennials *www.perennials.com*

Marion Jarvie *www.marionjarvie.ca*

Jim Lounsbery, Vineland Nurseries
www.vinelandnurseries.com/home.html

Jeff Mason, Mason House Gardens
www.masonhousegardens.com

Netherlands Flower Bulb Information Center *www.prod.bulbsonline.org/ibc/us_en/publiek/index.jsf*

Northscaping Inc., an Internet resource and community for landscapers and gardeners living in northern North America *www.northscaping.com*

Ellen Novack, writer
gardeningfromahammock@rogers.com

Perennial Resource
www.PerennialResource.com

Pine Knot Farms *www.pineknotfarms.com/*

Proven Winners *www.provenwinners.com*

Aldona Satterthwaite, Executive Director, Toronto Botanical Garden
www.torontobotanicalgarden.ca

Sheridan Nurseries
www.sheridannurseries.com

Wikimedia Commons
commons.wikimedia.org/wiki/

Paul Zammit, Director of Horticulture, Toronto Botanical Garden
www.torontobotanicalgarden.com

Photo Credits

Covers and Chapters

Front Cover: Dan Cooper;
Inside Front Cover: Kerria japonica, Jim Lounsbery;

Table of Contents – Caryopteris 'Summer Sorbet', Paul Zammit;

Introduction: p. 1 – Viburnum trilobum, Northscaping Inc.

Top Ten Plants
p. 3 – Alchemilla mollis, Athyrium nipponicum, Heritage Perennials

Chapter 1: p. 5 – Aldona Satterthwaite;
p. 6 – Gillenia trifoliata, – Echinacea purpurea 'Vintage Wine,' Paul Zammit; p. 7 – Monarda aquarius, Paul Zammit; p. 8 – Epimedium, Heritage Perennials

Chapter 2: p. 9 – Dan Cooper; p. 10 – Pulsatilla, Heritage Perennials; p. 11 – Astrantia, Heritage Perennials; p. 12 – Phlomis, Belinda Gallagher; Astilboides tabularis, Heritage Perennials

Chapter 3: p. 13 – Paul Zammit; p. 14 – Clematis, Dugald Cameron; Brunnera, Walters Gardens; p. 15 – Syringa, Dugald Cameron; p. 16 – Rosa, Dugald Cameron; – Dryopteris, Paul Zammit; p. 17 – Hygrangea serrata preziosa, Dugald Cameron; p. 18 – Berberis, Paul Zammit

Chapter 4: p. 19 – Marilyn Cornwell; p. 20 – Pinus, – Chionanthus, Marilyn Cornwell; – Fothergilla, Paul Zammit;
p. 22 – Crocosmia, Paul Zammit

Chapter 5: p. 23 – Paul Zammit; p. 24 – Vinca minor, Heritage Perennials; – Ilex, Paul Zammit; p. 25 – Euonymus, Paul Zammit; p. 26 – Cotoneaster, Heritage Perennials; – Pachysandra, Heritage Perennials

Chapter 6: p.27 – Paul Zammit; p. 28 – Thymus, Heritage Perennials; – Tricyrtis, Heritage Perennials; p. 30 – Heuchera, Paul Zammit

Chapter 7: p.31 – Perennial Resource; p. 32 – Salvia, Paul Zammit; – Ligularia, Heritage Perennials; p. 33 – Rudbeckia, Paul Zammit; – Carex, Heritage Perennials; p. 34 – Hosta, Heritage Perennials

Chapter 8: p.35 – Walters Gardens; p. 37 – Sambucus, Paul Zammit; – Hosta 'June,' – Aruncus, Heritage Perennials; p. 38 – Hydrangea, Paul Zammit

Chapter 9: p.39 – Lorraine Flanigan; p. 40 – Verbena, Heritage Perennials; p. 41 – Alchemila, Heritage Perennials; p. 42 – Geranium Rozanne, – Cimicifuga, Heritage Perennials; – Kirengeshoma, Paul Zammit

Chapter 10: p.43 – Marion Jarvie; p. 44 – Cornus, Paul Zammit; p. 46 – New Helleborus, Marion Jarvie; – Cornus, – Sedum, Walter Blonski

Chapter 11: p.47 – Marilyn Cornwell; p. 48 – Lavandula, Paul Zammit; p. 49 – Eryngium, Paul Zammit; – Aster, – Hosta, Heritage Perennials; p. 50 – Chasmanthium, Heritage Perennials

Chapter 12: p.51 – Dan Cooper; p. 52 – Sedum rupestre, Heritage Perennials; – Sedum sieboldii, Paul Zammit; p. 53 – Sedum telephium, Heritage Perennials; p. 54 – Sanguinaria, Paul Zammit; p. 55 – Athyrium, Paul Zammit; p. 56 – Adiantum, Heritage Perennials;

Chapter 13: p.57 – Paul Zammit; p. 58 – Euonymus, Northscaping; – Malus, Sheridan; p. 59 – Fothergilla (fall), Paul Zammit; p. 60 – Sagina, Heritage Perennials

Chapter 14: p.61 – Dan Cooper; p. 62 – Brassica, Paul Zammit; p. 63 – Chelone, Paul Zammit; – Hydrangea, Paul Zammit; – Athyrium, Heritage Perennials; p. 64 – Hachonechloa, Paul Zammit; – Papaver, Heritage Perennials

Chapter 15: p.65 – Paul Zammit; p. 66 – Hydrangea, – Caryopteris, Paul Zammit; – Iris, Heritage Perennials; p. 68 – Hachonechloa, Paul Zammit

Chapter 16: p.69 – Dan Cooper; p. 70 – Allium, Paul Zammit; p. 72 – Hydrangea, – Japanese anemone, Paul Zammit; – Hosta, Heritage Perennials

Chapter 17: p.73 – Marilyn Cornwell; p. 74 – Echinacea, Heritage Perennials; – Galium, Paul Zammit; p. 75 – Aruncus, – Hosta, Heritage Perennials

Botanical Reference Guide: p.77 – Perennial Resource

Botanical Reference Guide

Photo credits by placement in reference guide from beginning to end:

1, 4, 10, 36, 37, 38, 46, 53, 63, 125, 136, 152, 159, 172, 197, 266, 272, 276, 279, Sheridan Nurseries;

51, 131, 160, 256, Jim Lounsbery;

3, 52, 71, 104, 199, Walter Blonski;

2, 5, 6, 9, 13, 30, 31, 32, 47, 55, 64, 70, 86, 89, 95, 98, 100, 105, 106, 109, 116, 117, 121, 124, 129, 132, 146, 147, 148, 149, 150, 153, 154, 161, 166, 176, 205, 221, 224, 226, 227, 230, 241, 268, 274, 282, Paul Zammit;

7, 15, 16, 17, 18, 19, 20, 23, 24, 25, 26, 27, 29, 34, 40, 43, 44, 45, 48, 54, 57, 58, 62, 66, 74, 75, 80, 81, 82, 88, 91, 92, 93, 94, 99, 101, 102, 107, 108, 111, 112, 113, 114, 124, 127, 128, 134, 135, 137, 138, 139, 140, 143, 144, 145, 155, 156, 162, 164, 167, 168, 169, 170, 171, 174, 175, 180, 181, 185, 186, 187, 188, 189, 190, 192, 193, 194, 195, 206, 207, 208, 211, 222, 223, 232, 233, 235, 237, 239, 240, 242, 246, 247, 248, 249, 252, 257, 259, 260, 262, 271, 280, 281, Heritage Perennials;

8, 76, 179, 212, 261, 270, Netherlands Flower Bulb Information Center;

12, 49, 110, Jeff Mason;

14, Aquilegia discolor courtesy Ghislain118 (AD) http://www.fleurs-des-montagnes.net/;

21, 28, 33, 35, 78, 87, 133, 141, 195, 245, 251, 254, 263, Perennial Resource;

22, 67, 72, 79, 157, 202, 214, 215, 216, 217, 225, 234, 258, 264, Bailey Nurseries;

11, 69, 73, 85, 97, 115, 118, 119, 123, 198, 201, 213, 229, 238, 243, 244, 250, 265, 273, 275, 278, Northscaping Inc.;

12, Jeff Mason;

39, Hedwig Storch;

41, 122, I KENPEI;

42, 59, 163, 178, 184, 196, 231, Connon Nurseries and Northscaping Inc.;

50, Jerzy Opioła;

56, Marilyn Cornwell;

60, 65, 151, 218, 219, 256, Dugald Cameron;

68, 96, 204, 236, 253, 267, 277, Dan Cooper;

77, Bouba;

83, Richtid;

84, Wikimedia Commons;

103, Tortuosa;

126, Pine Knot Farms;

130, Marion Jarvie

158, 283, Ellen Novack;

165, Rosser1954

177, 190, Belinda Gallagher;

182, FoeNyx;

203, Kurt Stüber;

209, Georges Jansoone;

210, Pipi;

220, Daderot;

228, Kim Hansen